J. E. DAULE,
MULGRAVE,
LEYS DRIVE.

NEWNES POPULAR
HOME BOOK

VOL. I.

General Editor:
EDWARD MOLLOY

Advisory Editors:
A. C. HORTH, F.Coll.H., F.R.S.A.
L. B. HORTH

Chief Contributors to Vol. I.

A. C. HORTH, F.Coll.H., F.R.S.A.
JANE MASTERS
E. W. HOBBS
DAVID CHARLES
BASEDEN BUTT
JOAN HERRIN, A.R.C.A.
J. C. MacDERMOTT
Dr. F. W. ALEXANDER, M.R.C.S.,
    L.R.C.P. Edin., L.M., D.P.H. Eng.
Mrs. L. B. SYMONS

A. E. WATKINS
Mrs. L. B. HORTH
Capt. J. SACHS
S. JOHNSON, D.Sc.
W. G. CASE
KATHLEEN FIELDING
CHAS. H. HAYWARD
Mrs. M. C. PECKHAM
R. T. SHEARD
J. H. PECKHAM

GEORGE NEWNES, LIMITED,
SOUTHAMPTON STREET, LONDON, W.C. 2

PRINTED BY
WILLIAM CLOWES AND SONS, LIMITED,
DUKE STREET, STAMFORD STREET, LONDON, S.E. I.

PREFACE

THERE are two important problems in every-day life that make a strong appeal : one is connected with the home, its organisation and equipment, the other is concerned with a proper enjoyment of leisure hours. These two factors are so closely associated that it is difficult to separate them entirely.

The POPULAR HOME BOOK is intended to help the housewife especially, to make the best use of the household equipment, to carry out the necessary tasks by the most congenial and least laborious methods, to exercise that economy which in many cases is a necessity of modern life, and to keep herself and the members of her family in good health.

The HOME BOOK contains as well fully descriptive articles on useful crafts that will help in providing the home with greater comfort ; other articles deal with the more decorative crafts, to be applied to the beautifying of the home, to personal adornment, and to articles of utility.

For the housewife whose main interest is in the home, there are articles dealing with cleaning, cooking, furniture and furnishing, house decoration and repairs, emergencies and hints, labour saving, laundering, lighting and heating.

For the employment and enjoyment of leisure hours, especially for those who wish to employ their spare time profitably, many suggestions will be found in the large range of articles on craft subjects. These embrace all the decorative as well as utilitarian occupations that can be carried on in the home, and which do not require the use of specially equipped rooms.

The craft articles include simple pieces of work suitable for the beginner as well as more advanced designs for the practised worker. It will be possible by careful selection for a novice to gain a thorough practical knowledge of any particular craft.

The articles on beauty culture, health and exercise deal practically with the subjects and are intended mainly for the housewife who wishes to retain her health and vigour. The equally important problem of the health of every member of the family is dealt with by highly qualified and experienced medical men.

The articles dealing with craft subjects have been written by practising craft workers who, deft workers in their craft and gifted with the power of simple description, have explained in simple non-technical language the essential detail of their work.

The special attention of craft workers is drawn to the varied selection of useful and decorative crafts in this volume. These are designed to provide the beginner as well as the advanced worker with attractive and original examples. The articles dealing with Leather Work, Lamp Shade Making and Felt Applique are only a few of those suitable for the novice. The particularly attractive article on Hand-Weaving will, it is hoped, bring back to many homes that delightful craft.

The home handyman has not been forgotten, for there are articles on making shelves, a bookcase, a writing-desk, a carved wood candlestick, and a toy engine, and for the lover of the garden the article on Ornamental Cement and Concrete contains several most useful objects for adding to the beauty of the surroundings.

The photographic and other illustrations form a special feature of the HOME BOOK. Highly-skilled artists and photographers have co-operated with practical experts in producing not merely pictures, but pictorial descriptions of essential details designed to explain and amplify in the most lucid manner the important portions of the articles.

It is only by the loyal co-operation of contributors, artists, photographers and publishers, that the Editors have been able to present such a varied and comprehensive collection of useful and practical information. It is with confidence that we hope our efforts will bring pleasure and profit to our readers.

E. M.

L. B. H.

A. C. H.

CONTENTS OF VOL. I.

EVERY-DAY WORK IN THE HOME

FURNITURE AND FURNISHING

HEALTH AND HOME DOCTOR

HOUSE DECORATION AND REPAIRS

HOUSEHOLD EMERGENCIES AND HINTS

HOW TO KNOW

NEEDLECRAFTS

THINGS TO MAKE

THINGS TO MAKE—*(continued)*

WITH VOLUME I

CHART FOR THREE RUG DESIGNS.
CHART TO MAKE PANELLED VELLUM LAMP SHADE.
TRANSFER FOR EMBROIDERED TABLE CLOTH.
HOUSEHOLD CHART.
CHART TO MAKE CARVED WOOD CANDLE BRACKET.
TRANSFER FOR WOOL EMBROIDERED TEA-COSY.

EASY METHODS OF MAKING PILE RUGS

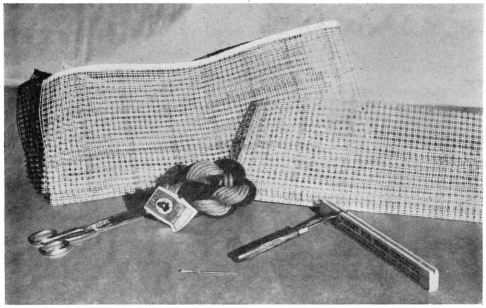

Fig. 1.—MATERIALS AND TOOLS REQUIRED FOR MAKING PILE RUGS.

The materials required consist of canvas and rug wool. The tools for ordinary pile rugs consist of a wool gauge and a catch hook, shown above, or spring nippers shown in Fig. 9. A needle is used when short pile rugs are to be made and a gauge of the kind illustrated in Fig. 14.

RUG-MAKING on canvas is not only a particularly fascinating and simple handicraft, but it is also a profitable occupation for the leisure hours requiring little initial outlay. There is a considerable amount of satisfaction to be obtained in making something that is really useful, and which, besides adding to the comfort of the home, provides opportunities for willing hands to help.

Although it is possible to buy many kinds of rugs in a large variety of patterns and colours, the particular shape and colour which would be most suitable is not always obtainable. By following one or other of the methods described in these pages, rugs may be made to fit any space and to harmonise with any colour scheme, besides being considerably less costly and more durable than the machine-made article.

How to Use the Rug-Making Chart

The designs on the rug-making Chart illustrate three different styles and indicate the possibilities in pleasing pattern and harmonious colour. They may be obtained ready stencilled on canvas, but the enlarged drafts enable the maker to follow out the pattern without much trouble by counting the squares. The drafts indicate also the method used in designing patterns and, by the use of squared paper, it is not difficult to invent new patterns. Experiments in colour schemes can be carried out on the squared paper, with crayons to represent the wools it is intended to use.

Three Methods of Rug-Making

There is a considerable choice in the methods of attaching the wool to the canvas. For producing the full pile rug there are several forms of hooks and other tools. Two popular tools are shown in Figs. 4 and 9. The short pile rug is done with a needle and is in many ways more economical in time and material.

Fig. 2.—PREPARING THE WOOL—FIRST OPERATION.
Lightly wind the wool round the gauge   It must not be stretched.

All the designs in the chart may be carried out in both methods as well as in cross-stitch. Instructions for making the latter form of rug will be described in a later article.

Materials Required—The Canvas

Canvas for rug-making is obtainable plain or with a coloured line dividing it up into large squares of eight holes to correspond with the charts. This makes the counting of the squares a very simple matter, and as it is also possible to obtain paper ruled out in the same manner, patterns may be worked out easily.

The canvas is available in 12, 18, 27, 36, 40, and 45-inch widths, the price varies from 1s. 6d. to 2s. 11d. per yard, according to width and quality. It is an advantage to use the material in the exact width required for the rug, as the selvedge will serve as the edge and avoids the necessity of turning in any of the canvas in finishing, except at the ends for which an allowance of about 4 inches should be made.

Rug Wool Required

There are so many excellent makes of rug wool obtainable that the selection is a matter of choice. The kind most generally used is a 6-ply yarn which is obtainable in a large range of colours. The rugs shown in the chart are designed specially for use with " Turkey " rug wool, and the quantities required for each colour are indicated.

In working out special designs, it is always advisable to obtain the whole of the wool required at first, as it may not be possible to match the exact shade afterwards. If it should be discovered when the rug is half made that there is insufficient wool to complete it, and no more of the original colour is available, the nearest should be obtained and the cut pieces mingled with the others so that the slight difference in not so noticeable.

Buy Good Quality Wool

The cheaper kinds of rug wool, however thick they are, generally contain more loose fluff than the dearer kinds and are therefore more liable to lose their body than those of the best quality, which are always preferable. Waste wool known as " thrums " can be used if economy must be studied, but its use gives more work, and great care is required to obtain an even texture. Although it is generally easier to use a 6-ply wool, two strands of

2-ply worked together makes a good texture.

AN ORDINARY PILE RUG

Cutting Strands of Wool to Size

In making the ordinary pile rug, it must be understood that the height of the pile depends on the size of the gauge used in cutting it into strands ready for tying to the canvas. An average size for the gauge is 1 inch wide and $\frac{1}{2}$ inch thick with a groove along one side, which is generally about $8\frac{1}{2}$ inches long. The makers of " Turkey " and " Beehive " wools supply a special gauge on which the quantities are based.

It is important that the cut pieces should be of equal length, so care should be taken to keep the strands even without overlapping and on no account should the wool be stretched or pulled when winding it on the gauge. Fig. 2 illustrates the way in which the wool is allowed to run easily through the fingers. The cutting may be done with a sharp knife run along the groove, but the use of scissors, as shown in Fig. 3, will be quite as satisfactory.

Using a Catch Hook

Of the methods described, the first is carried out with a special tool fitted with a catch which prevents the point of the hook catching in the canvas when it is pulled through the mesh. Although the simple form of catch hook illustrated in Fig. 1 is efficient and quite inexpensive, a saving of time is possible with the "Eric" self-opening spring latch hook.

First Stage

The first stage in knotting the strand of wool is shown in Fig. 4, and consists in pushing the hook through a mesh so that the catch is carried past a double strand through a hole in the next row, leaving the hook open. A strand of the wool is picked up in the left hand, exactly doubled, and the loop slipped over the hook and drawn tight as indicated.

Completing the Tuft

The hook is now pulled through the two holes (see Fig. 5) for about half the length of the strand, and it will be seen that the catch will fall over and cover the point of the hook, thus allowing it to pass the strands of the canvas. The slight tension necessary to keep the wool straight is now relaxed and the hook pushed through the loop and caught in the doubled strand (see Fig. 6). A firm and steady pull on the hook will draw the double strand through the loop, as indicated at Fig. 7. The knot, as shown at Fig. 8, is tightened up by a steady tug of the fingers.

This sequence of operations takes very little time, and with continual practice a high speed will soon be attained.

Using Spring Nippers

An exactly similar result is obtainable by using spring nippers instead of a hook. The method is quite simple and consists in first picking up a strand and passing the end of the nippers through the loop. The point of the nippers is now pushed through one hole to the next, the loop of wool being behind and on top of the canvas (Fig. 9).

The next stage consists in opening the jaws of the nippers by a light pressure of the thumb and inserting the cut ends of the strand, as

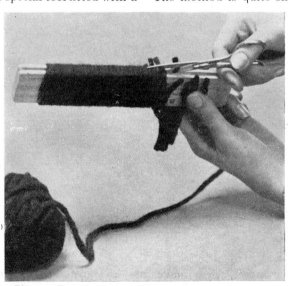

Fig. 3.—PREPARING THE WOOL—SECOND OPERATION
Cutting the wool into strands of uniform length.

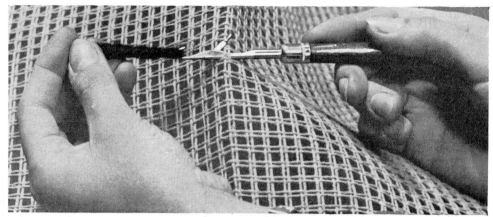

Fig. 4.—MAKING THE TUFTS OF AN ORDINARY PILE RUG USING A CATCH HOOK—FIRST STAGE.
Push the hook under the canvas mesh as shown.   Double the strand of wool
and attach the loop to the hook.

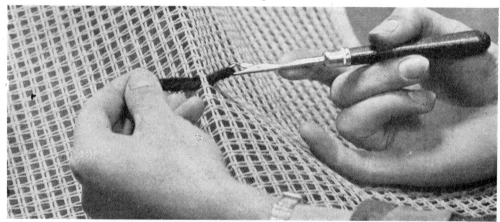

Fig. 5.—TUFTING—SECOND STAGE.
Pull the wool through the two holes in the canvas.

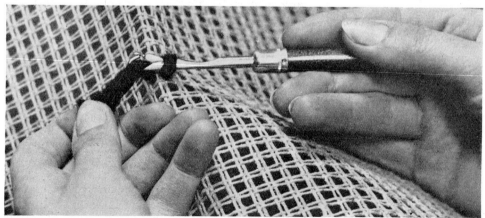

Fig. 6.—TUFTING—THIRD STAGE.
Now push the hook through the loop of the wool and catch the doubled strand.

Fig. 7.—FOURTH STAGE.

Pull the doubled strand through its loop, so making a knot.

on the canvas in order to ascertain if the correct number of squares have been filled up.

It is a matter of individual choice as to the method of working out the pattern. Some workers prefer to work across the horizontal rows and fill in the colours of the pattern as they come for a depth of 2 or 3 inches and then complete the background. Others work from the centre and outline the pattern, one knot all round. The space inside the outline is then filled up and finally the background is filled row by row.

It is always better to work in one direction, preferably from right to left, so that the pile can be kept quite even. When the last inch or so remains, the canvas should be turned up and the last row filled in. It is easier to complete the rug in this way as the doubled canvas is difficult to bend.

Finishing Off

In finishing off the rug after the last knot has been made, it may be necessary to use a large pair of scissors to clip off uneven lengths. The whole of the surface should now be thoroughly rubbed with the hand to remove the fluff. Some experts use a comb for collecting the

shown in Fig. 10. The pressure on the spring is now relaxed so that the wool is secured. Finally, the tool is drawn backwards through the hole and the loop and pulled tight to form the knot, as shown in Fig. 11. This method forms the knot in one operation, and although it takes a little longer at first, many rug-makers find they are able to use this tool much more quickly than the hook.

As there will be a considerable number of strands needed for a pile rug, it is a good plan to keep the wool separately in shallow boxes so that the stock of cut strands may be renewed at odd moments. Wool gauges can be obtained mounted in a stand and fitted with a handle so that time may be saved in winding, they are quite inexpensive.

How to Work

Having decided on a particular design and a method of work, the canvas, cut to size with an allowance for turning in at the ends, is placed conveniently on the knees or on a table with one end immediately in front. Turn up an inch or so and begin the first row of knots through the double canvas. The chart should be close at hand for constant reference, and is needed even if the design is stencilled

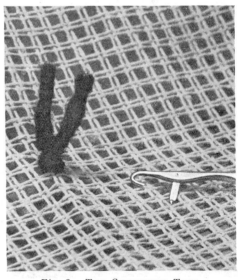

Fig. 8.—THE COMPLETED TUFT.

When the knot has been made, tighten it.

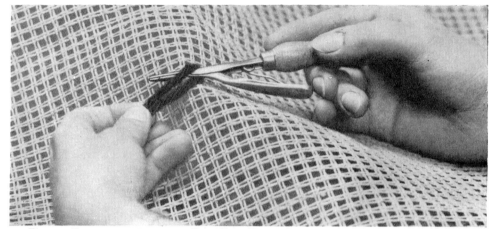

Fig. 9.—TUFTING AN ORDINARY PILE RUG USING SPRING NIPPERS—FIRST OPERATION.
Pass the end of the nippers through the loop of a doubled wool strand, and then through two
holes in the mesh of the canvas.

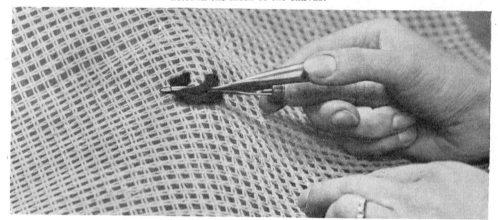

Fig. 10.—USING SPRING NIPPERS—SECOND OPERATION.
Nip hold of the ends of the wool in the jaws of the nippers.

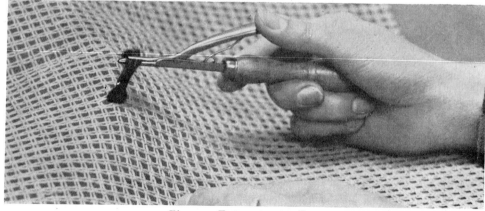

Fig. 11.—FINISHING THE TUFT.
Pull the ends of the wool through the loop. This will knot the tuft to the canvas.

finished ; in fact, it is preferable to leave it unlined, as it is easier to keep it free from dust. The better plan is to sew a strip of ordinary webbing along the canvas. It is an advantage to insert a small piece of sheet lead at the corners ; the overlap of the webbing may be used to form a pocket for the weight.

SHORT PILE RUG

The Method

The short pile rug is made by an entirely different method and uses less wool. The stitches are knotted to the canvas, but instead of a hook and short lengths of wool, a large needle is used with a gauge, which may be a pencil, for example. Any of the designs on the

Fig. 12.—MAKING A
SHORT PILE RUG—
FIRST STAGE.

Pass the needle threaded with wool downwards through the lower of the two horizontal strands. Then pass the needle downwards underneath the upper strand.

fluff, but considerable care is needed with this tool to avoid undue strain on the fibres. It is almost impossible to rub out all the fluff at first, but a rub over the surface occasionally after the rug is in use will gradually clean it.

Lining not Necessary

It is not necessary to line the rug when

Fig. 13.—SHORT PILE RUG—SECOND STAGE.
Draw the wool through and pull lightly to form the above knot.

How to Work

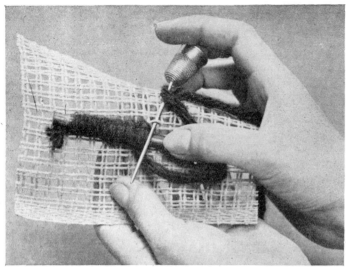

Fig. 14.—MAKING SHORT PILE RUG—THIRD STAGE.

Working from the stage reached in Fig. 13, place the gauge on the canvas and bring the wool under and over it. Insert needle under the lower strand of the next mesh and then under the top strand as shown.

The canvas should be placed on a table with the row to be worked resting on the edge, a weight being placed on the remainder to keep it in position. The needle should be threaded with a length of wool about a yard long. Begin by passing the needle downwards through the lower of the first two horizontal threads, leaving an inch or two of the end. Holding the free end firmly, pass the needle downwards underneath the upper of the two strands (Fig. 12). The wool is now drawn through and pulled lightly to form the knot (*see* Fig. 13).

The gauge is now placed on the canvas and the needle is passed under and over

chart, and those for tufted rugs generally, can be copied by this method. Short pile rugs require only two-thirds the amount of wool necessary for long pile rugs.

Wool

The wool used in the short pile rug is generally 6-ply, but the method lends itself to the use of a more lustrous wool. The effect approximates more closely to that of the Persian rug, especially if the design is traditional. The canvas used is a little coarser and has thicker strands than that used for the hook method, otherwise it is similar in appearance.

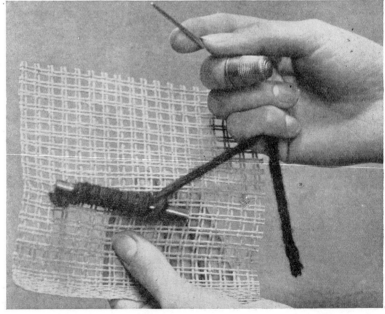

Fig. 15.—FOURTH STAGE.

Draw the wool through ready for bringing it under and over gauge again.

the gauge, and then under the lower thread of the next mesh so that the wool is on the left of the needle. The wool is now drawn through and the needle threaded under the upper strand, so that the wool is on the right, as shown in Fig. 14. Pull through and draw up tight, as indicated in Fig. 15, when the stitch is complete. The row is completed in this way.

When the length of wool is finished, cut the end to the same length as the size of the gauge. New lengths are started in the same way and, when approaching the end of the gauge, slip off some of the loops on the left and push it along. In beginning the pattern after the outside border has been done, it is better to work straight across the canvas from left to right. This keeps the work even and the canvas straight. But the pattern may be completely worked out and the background fitted in afterwards.

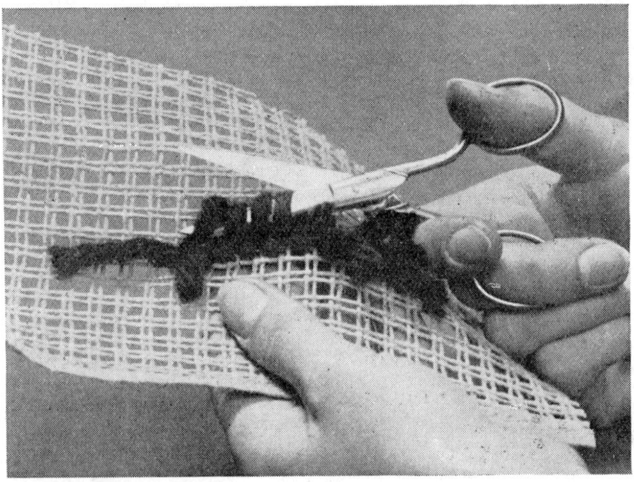

Saving Time

The different colours as they occur in the design are begun by the same stitch as the beginning stitch of a row and the end cut off to the gauge length. Time is saved by using as many needles as there are colours in the design ; this avoids constantly threading the same needle, as in some patterns the separate lengths may be quite short.

The loops when completed should be cut with scissors (see Fig. 16). Some workers cut the loops after a length or so of the gauge has been worked ; others

leave it until a row is finished or until all the rows have been completed. It is advisable if the work is done only in odd moments to cut the loops as the work proceeds, as they are liable to be pressed out of position, and this renders cutting rather troublesome.

Finishing the Rug

The rug should be trimmed on the surface with scissors to remove any irregular strands and then rubbed over and thoroughly shaken to remove the fluff. The ends of the canvas are turned back and covered underneath with webbing to complete.

Fig. 16.—COMPLETING TUFTS OF SHORT PILE RUG.
Slip the gauge from the loops and cut as shown.

Working from the Chart

The above instructions apply to all the special designs shown in the large chart. Each square on the enlarged draft represents a stitch and there is one stitch for every ridge in the canvas. To be successful, Patons and Baldwins' canvases, wool and gauges should be used, as they correspond exactly with the draft. The canvas has a coloured thread every eight squares to correspond with the thick lines on the chart.

The semi-circular design which is easily adaptable to make a circular rug is shown in a blue scheme on the draft together with a suitable range of colours. The modernistic design is particularly effective in the brown scheme. The appliqué design is a good example of an association of colours that will fit in with almost any scheme. Readers should have no difficulty in selecting from these three designs one which will suit their requirements.

An Interesting Fact About Curtains

Cretonne curtains, in spite of light wallpaper and paint, tend to keep a room dark if the window is screened by buildings or trees.

Muslin curtains not only help in screening the view, they also distribute the light. Note the difference.

AN EASILY-MADE SET OF LUNCHEON MATS

WORKED IN COLOURED WOOLS

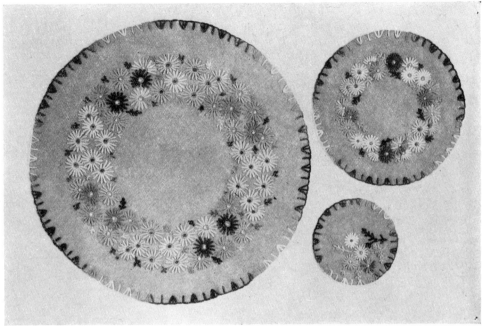

Fig. I.—ATTRACTIVE AND COLOURFUL WOOL EMBROIDERED LUNCHEON MATS.
No difficulty should be experienced in making and embroidering these useful and decorative
table mats if the accompanying instructions are followed.

EMBROIDERY has once more become a fashionable occupation for all. Not only are women to be found busily intent upon decorative stitchery, but men, too, and at recent exhibitions of this class of work, it was noticeable that many of the most successful specimens were the product of masculine skill.

Readers who are new to needlework will do well to start with very simple forms, so as not to be disheartened. Wool embroidery is ideal for them, for the stitches are easy and so quickly carried out, while the results are out of all proportion to the time and money expended.

Take the alluring set of luncheon mats illustrated in Fig. I. This was worked in a few hours and the cost was trifling.

Stitches to Use

The set is worked entirely in stroke-stitch, and French knots, with the edges blanket-stitched. Every flower is worked in the same way, but monotony is avoided by the skilful arrangement of colours.

Materials Required

In the original a pale leaf-green linen was used for the foundation, while embroidery wool was used for the working in four shades each of blue, mauve, yellow and pink, with two shades of green and black. Shaded green wool was used for the edges.

To make a set consisting of a large centre mat, four plate mats, and four glass mats, you need ¾ yard of linen 36 inches wide, one skein of wool in each of the colours mentioned, except the shaded green wool, of which four balls will be needed. The centre mat should measure 16 inches in diameter, the plate mats 9 inches in diameter, and the glass ones 5 inches.

Copying the Design on to the Linen

Readers may copy the designs to be embroidered on to the linen by the method of "pouncing" shown on page 13. A set of

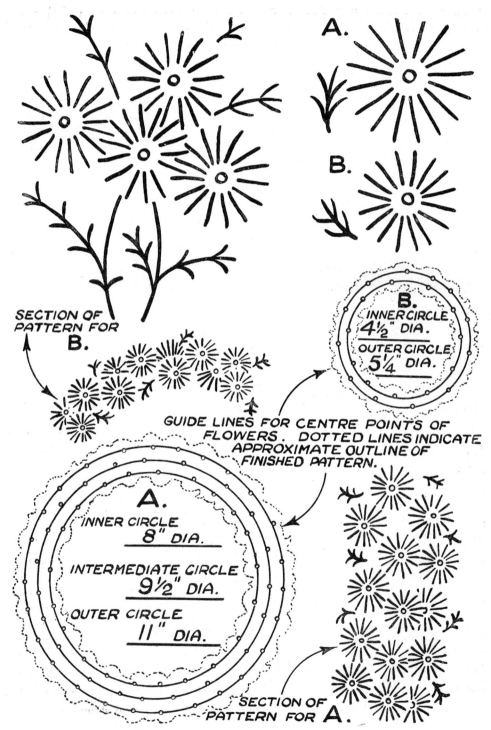

A.

B.

SECTION OF
PATTERN FOR
B.

B.
INNER CIRCLE
4½" DIA.
OUTER CIRCLE
5¼" DIA.

GUIDE LINES FOR CENTRE POINTS OF
FLOWERS. DOTTED LINES INDICATE
APPROXIMATE OUTLINE OF
FINISHED PATTERN.

A.
INNER CIRCLE
8" DIA.

INTERMEDIATE CIRCLE
9½" DIA.

OUTER CIRCLE
11" DIA.

SECTION OF
PATTERN FOR A.

Fig. 2.—DESIGN DETAILS FOR THE MATS.

Fig. 3.—THE FIRST STAGE IN POUNCING.
After tracing the design on strong tracing paper, use a fine pricker to prick out the design from the back of the tracing paper. Notice the felt pad underneath.

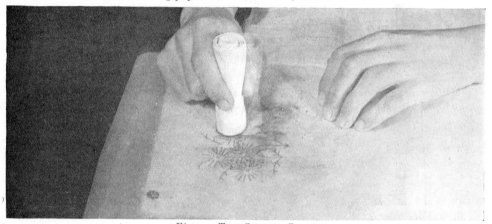

Fig. 4.—THE SECOND STAGE.
Next fix the tracing on to the linen by drawing pins, and use a pad dipped in powdered charcoal to rub the design through the perforations in the tracing paper.

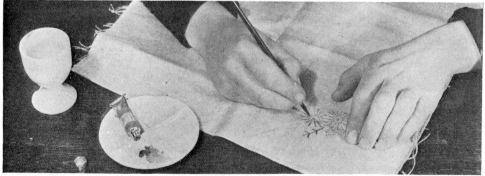

Fig. 5.—THE THIRD STAGE.
Now use light red water-colour and paint over the lines of the design as shown. The above method may be used for any pattern and is particularly useful where the same design has to be repeated many times.

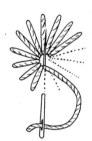

Fig. 6.—Simple Stroke-Stitch for Flowers.

transfers may be obtained for the designs or they may be drawn from the details on page 12 where are shown clearly the units used and the method of building up the three designs.

With plates or compasses mark out the necessary circles in pencil on the linen and leave as large a space round each as possible. Transfer the designs in the middle of the centre mat and plate mats, and to one side of each small mat.

Work the embroidery of all mats before cutting any out, as a small piece of linen is uncomfortable to hold in the hand.

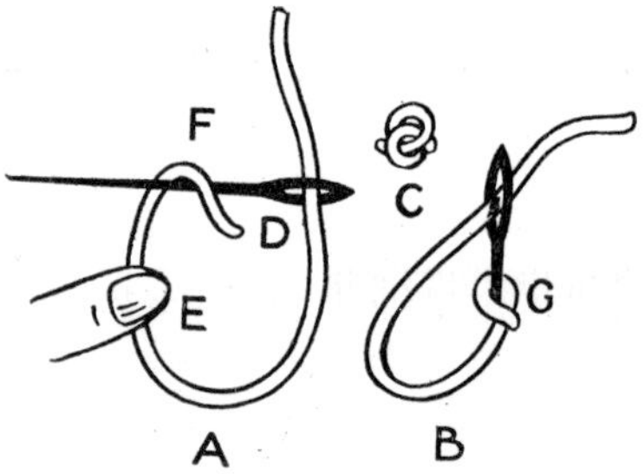

The Plate Mats

There are 24 flowers on each wreath of the plate mat, and each group of three is worked in a different colour, thus :—
First group, pink ; second group, mauve ; third group, yellow ; fourth group, blue. Then repeat the colours in the same order. Each flower in the group is worked in a different shade. The stitch is simply stroke-stitch, bringing up the needle at the outside edge and putting it back on the inner. It is best to pass the needle upwards and downwards through the linen to avoid pulling the wool.

Make a French knot in the middle of each flower, twisting the wool only once round the needle. Use black knots on pink and yellow flowers, and yellow on blue and mauve. Work the little leaf sprays in stroke-stitch in the two shades of green alternately.

The Centre Mat

There are 56 flowers in this wreath. With pins divide them into eight groups of seven flowers each, and work each group in a different

colour, in the order given for the first mat. As each group has seven flowers instead of three, make two in the dark shade, three in the medium, and two in the light. Separate the shades as much as possible.

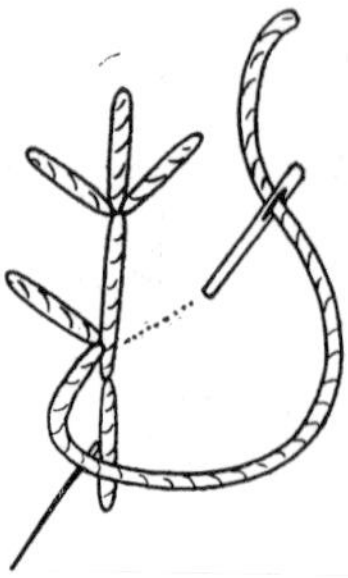

The Glass Mats

The spray has four flowers, so work each one in a different colour, using whichever shade you prefer. Use the two shades of green for the stems.

Pressing

When the embroidery is finished, place the work on a thick blanket with its right side downwards. Lay a wet cloth on the back and press the background heavily with a warm iron, but only press very lightly on the embroidery. The background should be really wet. Remove the wet cloth and press the background until dry.

Then take green sewing-cotton and run finely round the pencilled circle of each mat. Do not draw the stitches up at all. Cut round the mats, leaving a $\frac{1}{4}$-inch turning. Turn this down and tack carefully, being careful not to stretch the edge—the running is a precaution against this. Press the edges lightly on the wrong side.

Neatening the Edges

Work round the edges with fancy blanket-stitch. First comes a group of three stitches all worked into the same hole, then a space and a single stitch, then another space, then three stitches again, and so on. When bringing out the needle at the edge of the mat,

Fig. 7.—Stroke Stitch for Sprays.

Fig. 8.—French Knots for Flower Centres.

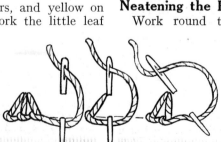

Fig. 9.—Blanket-Stitch for Borders.

catch it through the linen to keep the loop firm.

On the centre mat make the stitches $\frac{1}{2}$-inch deep, on the plate mats $\frac{3}{8}$ inch, and on the glass mats $\frac{1}{4}$ inch.

Press the edges lightly with a warm iron but no damp cloth.

These same three transfers can be used most effectively for a bedspread. Make this of linen with hemmed edges worked with chain-stitch in wool. Place the bedspread on the bed, take one large wreath transfer, four small wreaths and four sprays, and pin them in position.

The large wreath should go in the middle, four small wreaths round it, and the small sprays in between.

Another Method of Working

If any reader has a large quantity of odd lengths of wool she need not stick to the colour scheme given here. The colours can be used promiscuously, and the more shades used the better, as long as two flowers of the same shade never come together, and the colours are nicely distributed.

How to Lay a Fire
SHOWING THE RIGHT AND WRONG WAYS

Fig. 1.—This is not the best way of laying a fire. The paper spread out on the bottom of the grate prevents the updraught necessary for good burning.

Fig. 2.—The paper should be torn up and crumpled up. The wood should be broken up into short lengths.

Fig. 3.—Place the wood as shown in this illustration.

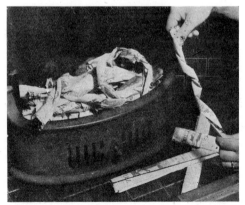

Fig. 4.—Paper folded into strips and twisted will be sufficient without wood.

BEAUTY CULTURE

CARE OF THE FACE AND COMPLEXION

THE lines which appear on the face are caused by the action of the facial muscles, and the expression given to the face varies with the muscles which are thrown into action, and may be anything from delight to horror.

Lines that Make One Old

CROWS FEET are formed by the action of a circular muscle round the eye.

FINE LINES ROUND THE MOUTH are formed by a circular muscle round the mouth.

TRANSVERSE LINES ON THE FOREHEAD are formed by a muscle attached to the skin at the level of the eyeball and which runs up over the forehead.

VERTICAL LINES between the eyebrows are formed by a small muscle lying under the circular muscle of the eye and running from the root of the nose to the inner end of the eyebrow.

Round the mouth are two sets of radiating muscles, the upper and lower, the upper are the muscles of Comedy, the lower of Tragedy.

Laugh—and Keep Young

To appreciate the effect of the facial muscles, sit in front of a well-lighted mirror with the diagram, Fig. 1, at hand, assume an expression of utter misery and go through all the varying grades of possible expression, working up to laughter, noting the muscles which come into play and the lines which appear. It is clear then that the contours of the face

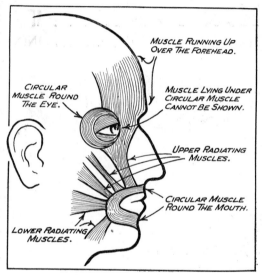

CIRCULAR MUSCLE ROUND THE EYE.

MUSCLE RUNNING UP OVER THE FOREHEAD.

MUSCLE LYING UNDER CIRCULAR MUSCLE CANNOT BE SHOWN.

UPPER RADIATING MUSCLES.

CIRCULAR MUSCLE ROUND THE MOUTH.

LOWER RADIATING MUSCLES.

*Fig. 1.—*MUSCLES WHICH ARE RESPONSIBLE FOR THE FACE LINES.

The action of these muscles tend to form lines on the face. Knowledge of these will assist in counteracting those lines which are not desired.

are to a large extent affected by the attitude of mind. In everyday life, the muscles are unconsciously used and the varying moods are reflected in the face, so it is evident that a sulky, discontented disposition will develop sullen, while the cheerful and philosophical, pleasant lines.

The muscles tend to sag with age, but frequent action of the upper lifting muscles (i.e., the comedy muscles) help to counteract this, so those who laugh at care will wear better than those who meet troubles half-way. Lines will come, but at least they can be pleasant ones.

TAKING CARE OF THE COMPLEXION

Cleansing

In order that the skin may function properly the face must be as carefully cleaned as the rest of the body. Soap and water is not necessarily the best medium, if soap is used it should not be highly-scented or strong. The best method to adopt is to apply cold cream immediately after the evening bath, which will have opened the pores of the skin. Work the cream well in with the tips of the fingers with a circular movement, starting at the chin and working up over the face lightly and without pressure, going carefully into the groove in the chin and those at the side of the nostrils, but not working over the eyelid or in the socket under the eye. If make-up has been used on the eyes, remove it very carefully and gently with warm olive or

Fig. 2.—IF THE DISPOSITION IS CHEERFUL.

Only pleasing lines will develop.

tips of the two middle fingers from below upwards ; it should be applied evenly and smoothly, leaving no definite line. Remember that the powder will tone the rouge down slightly, but guard against over-rouging. The position for the rouge varies according to the individual characteristics of the face, and experiments should be made in front of a mirror.

Powdering

Apply powder of a tint to tone in with the skin. The correct way to apply powder is as follows : Take a piece of medicated gauze about 6 inches square, lay it flat on the table, place in

almond oil. Then gently but firmly wipe off the cream with a soft cloth or cleansing tissue (which can be bought at any chemists at a very small cost), working from chin upwards and so removing dirt and all make-up. Again smear the face freely with cold cream and massage as before, but this time exert a little upward pressure, gently wipe off all superfluous cream. In the morning wash with warm water, a little soap may be used if desired. Bathe well with cold or practically cold water and dry with light friction.

Make-up

First work in a foundation cream, then apply the rouge very lightly, working it in with the

Fig. 3.—AN EMBITTERED DISPOSITION CANNOT BUT DEVELOP UNPLEASANT LINES ON THE FACE.

Remember, a woman is as old as she looks, and she looks as old as the lines on her face.

the centre a small, flat piece of cotton-wool, lap the two sides over, then tuck in the ends; this will make a compact pad. Dip the pad in the powder and dab the powdered side over the face with a light, tapping movement, carefully remove all superfluous powder, leaving a light even film.

Spare the Lipstick

Lipstick should be used sparingly and the contour of the mouth followed ; the lower lip should hardly be coloured at all and the colour on both lips should be worked in with the tip of the little finger.

Pencilling the Eyebrows

If the eyebrows are very fair they may be lightly pencilled : for ordinary every-day purposes the eyelashes should be left untouched.

Cleansing Specially Sensitive Skins

Strictly speaking, soap should not be used on the face, but it is permissible unless ill-effects result, i.e., blotches and roughness, when water and no soap may be tried. If the blotches persist, entirely give up the use of water on the face; use warm English almond oil and dab the whole face and eyes in the morning with a pad, made as directed above, moistened with equal parts of witch-hazel and water, a bottle of which may be kept ready mixed. Proceed with the make-up.

A Weekly Skin Treatment

Prepare several pads as directed, cleanse the face thoroughly with cold cream or almond oil as directed in the nightly treatment.

Massage

When all the cleansing agent has been removed, dip the tips of the second, third and fourth fingers in warm almond oil, and, starting at the middle of the chin, massage gently but firmly, working along the lines of the muscles with an upward pressure, bearing in mind Fig. 1. Re-dip the fingers as the oil becomes absorbed. The whole of the face should be massaged except the eyelids and eyesockets. When working on the flesh just under the cheekbone,

hold the flesh just under the eyesocket and along the line of the cheekbone with the fingers of one hand while massaging with the other, this prevents any dragging of the very delicate tissue under the eye. At least ten minutes should be devoted to this massage.

Carefully wipe off all the oil with a pad, take another pad and dip it in an astringent lotion made up as follows :— 1 pint of elderflower water, 15 drops of tincture of benzoin, 1 teaspoonful of *eau-de-Cologne*. This mixture should be bottled and a little poured into a small receptacle. Keep the bottle in a cool, dark place. The pad should be just saturated, but no more. Hold one end of it between the fingers and thumb and gently, but briskly, slap the face. Begin at the chin and work up over the cheeks, nose and forehead, avoiding the eye-sockets, which may be gently wiped. This movement should be continued until the whole face is thoroughly moistened, then gently pat with a soft, smooth towel until the face is quite dry, then proceed with make-up as usual.

Eyes

Where soap and water is not used on the face, the eyes should be carefully cleansed with a witch-hazel and water solution (half and half) by means of a small pad, but bear in mind that the skin round the eyes is extremely delicate and will only stand very gentle treatment. Once a week or more frequently use a weak boracic eyebath.

TREATMENT OF BLEMISHES

Blackheads

Greasy skins are liable to these, caused by choking of the pores, because the fat glands are over-active and their excretion solidifies in the opening, filling the pores with a suety substance. The blackhead is formed by dirt adhering.

Apply a Hot Fomentation

Apply a hot fomentation to the place affected, as follows : Place a strip of white cotton or linen material in a small basin, with the ends of the strip hanging down over the sides ; cut a strip of boracic lint and fold in several thicknesses so that it will be such a size as to well cover the blackhead, and, placing it on the cloth on the bottom of the basin, pour on it a small quantity of boiling water. Take an end of the cloth in each hand and wring until the lint is as dry as possible. Apply the lint to the affected part. This should be repeated until the area round the blackhead is thoroughly softened, then cover the two first fingers with a small piece of gauze and gently press out the blackhead. Press between the pads at the tip of the fingers so that the nails do not come in contact with the skin. The blackhead and the suety substance will ooze out and must be wiped away with wet boracic lint, then apply a pad dipped in cold water to close the pores, and pat with astringent lotion. This should be done at night after the usual cleansing.

Fig. 4.—FACE MASSAGE.
Starting at the chin, work along the lines of the muscles, which are shown in Fig. 1, except round the eyes.

Acne and its Treatment

Acne is an infection of the oil glands by the acne bacillus. It is usually found in greasy skins and frequently in or around a blackhead. The germ gains entrance and grows on the oily material, and produces a poison which gives rise to an inflamed swelling, in the centre of which appears a yellow spot ; a good deal of pain may result.

In the early stages the application of alcohol on a small piece of cotton-wool (pure alcohol should be used) may help to destroy the germ, but no pressure must be given until the yellow head is well formed, then apply a hot fomentation as directed in the treatment for blackheads, dip a darning needle in boiling water, and with the point puncture the centre of the yellow head, press out the yellow substance as directed in the case of the blackhead. Do not let the contents

Fig. 5.—WHEN MASSAGING UNDER THE CHEEKBONE.
Hold the flesh at the cheekbone with one hand and massage with the other.

2—2

of the spot come in contact with the skin, but wipe away with wet boracic lint to prevent the infection spreading, using fresh lint each time and covering the fingers with fresh lint for each spot. When the spot is cleared, touch the cavity with the tip of a pointed orange stick which has been covered with cotton-wool and dipped in hydrogen peroxide, then apply a dusting powder. It should be remembered that acne is highly infectious, and the pus will most probably infect any part of the skin with which it comes in contact; it is difficult to cure and liable to scar badly.

Prevention of Acne

Prevention is, therefore, much better than cure. A sulphur soap may be used, also a sulphur ointment. Skins liable to acne will stand any amount of friction, and to keep them in condition when there are no actual spots, apply a little spirit soap to a wet square of flannel and cleanse the face with this; rinse thoroughly first with warm and then with cold water, dry and use dusting powder. Before make-up is used, such skins may have a little thin calamine lotion applied instead of the usual foundation cream. Pay attention to diet, avoid rich food and take plenty of exercise and keep the bowels well open. Remember that if the skin of the face is greasy, the oil glands all over the body will also be over-active; it is, therefore, important that all the cleansing instructions should be followed very carefully, and plenty of friction given both in washing and drying. Sulphur soap and ointment and spirit soap may be obtained from any chemist.

Treating Dry Patches

When the skin is liable to these, the face should never be washed with water, but warm almond oil should be used and Crookes Collosol Sulphur Bath applied to the patches when they appear. This may be bought at the chemist's and a little, diluted with water (half and half), dabbed on each patch after cleansing. The use of salt in the diet should be

Fig. 6.—Preventing Double Chin.

An upward stroking movement for massaging the neck and under the chin. A later article will deal more fully with massage.

avoided and if the patches persist consult a doctor.

Enlarged Pores

Every day use an astringent lotion, following the directions given for its use in the weekly treatment.

HOW TO APPLY A MUD PACK

Unless the skin is very dry, a mud pack

may be given about once a month. Mix two tablespoonfuls of fuller's earth to a smooth paste with boiling water and stand over a saucepan of boiling water to keep hot.

First—A Hot Towel

Cleanse the face, following the directions already given, wring a small towel out of boiling water and hold it over the face ; the towel should be as hot as can be borne without scalding ; this is to open the pores.

Applying the Paste

Remove the towel and quickly apply the paste, starting at the chin. Take a little of the paste up on the back of a small wooden spoon and smooth it on to the face ; work in this way up over the face until all but the eyesockets, nostrils and lips are covered. The pack should be as hot as can be comfortably borne and should be left on until nearly dry.

While Pack is Drying

While the pack is drying, sit in a reclining position or lie down. The eyes may be covered with pieces of cotton-wool damped with wych-hazel. The restful position is part of the treatment.

Washing Off

When the pack is nearly dry wash off the paste with cold water, be sure that all

is removed and continue bathing the face until all crevices are quite clear. The cold water will close the pores. Dry the face and lightly smear with cold cream. It is best to give this treatment at night, just before going to bed. As some of the paste may drop while it is being applied, a washing dressing-jacket or gown should be worn.

A Pack for Dry Skins

Mix 1 dessertspoonful of fine oatmeal with 2 tablespoonfuls of cold milk, stir in 1 medicine glass of boiling milk, stir this mixture over heat until it thickens, then stir in 1 teaspoonful of almond oil. Prepare the face and apply the mixture, following the directions given for the mud pack, only wash off with milk instead of water. This may be done once a month.

Both these mixtures will tend to thicken if kept hot for long. If they become too thick for easy application, they may be thinned, the mud with a little hot water and the oatmeal with hot milk.

SUNBURN

Preventing

An oily skin will stand almost any amount of sun and benefit by it, but a dry skin should be carefully protected. Thin calamine lotion may be applied as a preventative and will help to allay the pain and irritation after burning has taken place.

ENAMELLING THE TAPS

OLD-FASHIONED water taps can be enamelled quite successfully provided that every trace of dirt and grease is removed by washing with hot soda water. Then brighten all the metal parts by rubbing with emery paper, brush off the dust and then apply the porcelain enamel with soft brush.

Special enamels are sold for this purpose and should be flowed on generously, allowed to dry hard and a second coat then applied.

WIRELESS ACCUMULATORS

SIMPLE NOTES WHICH WILL HELP YOU TO AVOID TROUBLE

HOW often do you say, "Oh! for an accumulator on which I can depend"? You need never experience the disappointment of not being able to use your receiver through a faulty accumulator if you read the following hints carefully :—

Many of the troubles in accumulators are due to corrosion. How many terminals have you seen fast disappearing and becoming a sticky mass ? Yet this can easily be prevented if care is taken.

When the accumulator is taken off charge or received back from the charging station, do not straightaway connect to the receiver, but give it a good clean, for during charging, gassing and spraying of the acid takes place and condenses on the outside and terminals. Remove the terminals, but if they are tight do not force with a pair of pliers or the result may be a broken terminal.

How to Loosen a Tight Terminal

The following is the correct way, and no matter how the terminal may be corroded it can be removed with the fingers. Firstly, if the case is of celluloid, carefully cover the top well round the terminal with a wet rag ; now make a piece of iron well hot and hold on to the top of the terminal. When the terminal is quite hot you will find it will unscrew with the fingers (holding the terminal with a rag, for it will be hot). If the terminals are of the insu-

lated type, do not use the hot iron—the only way, with this type of terminal, is to use a rag soaked in very hot water and placed well over the terminal.

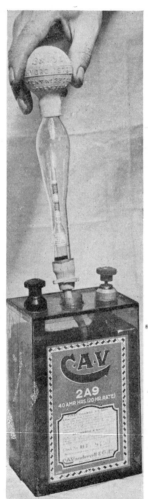

Fig. i.—USING THE HYDROMETER.
A little acid is drawn up into the tube and a reading taken on the inner float. A fully charged battery should read from 1250-1300. If the reading is below 1150 the battery needs recharging immediately.

Cleaning the Accumulator Case

After removing the terminals, carefully clean the sides and top with a rag well damped with strong soda water or ammonia—this will kill the acid. It is very important that care is taken to see that the soda does not enter the inside of the accumulator, or the acid will be spoilt. There is little fear of this happening so long as the vent plugs are not removed.

The terminal nuts should be placed right in the soda or ammonia and afterwards well dried and cleaned.

The accumulator should now have a nice clean and dry appearance.

The terminal must now be covered with petroleum jelly or vaseline.

Good, sound and clean contact at the terminals of the accumulator is one of the secrets of freedom from crackle and the correct voltage on the valves.

We will now give attention to the inside, as the condition of the plates must be watched, for the life and service of the accumulator depends upon the care taken ; it is no use expecting the charging station to do this for you, because the trouble may start developing while the accumulator is in your charge ; more so if the interval between the chargings are long. It is a wise and economical plan to have accumulators re-charged every two or three weeks, even when they are not in use, as accumulators, when left standing will become discharged, and if left in this condition for long the plates will quickly sulphate and the accumulator is then only fit for scrapping. The interval between charging will depend on the size of the accumulator and the number of valves it has to run ; if it is a small cell it may require charging every week.

The appearance of the plates should be as follows :—

" Positive," a chocolate-brown.
" Negative," a grey colour.

Fig. 2.—REMOVING A TIGHT TERMINAL.
First protect the celluloid by means of a wet rag, as shown.

White Patches on the Plates

If it is noticed that white patches are occurring on the positive plates, sulpha-tion is taking place, and is due to either the accumula-tor being dis-charged too low, or having been left

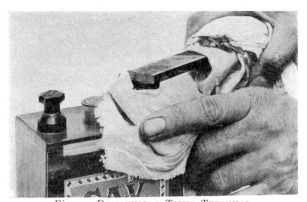

Fig. 3.—REMOVING A TIGHT TERMINAL.
Next apply a hot iron to the top of the terminal. This will expand it so that it can be unscrewed easily.

standing in a discharged condition. Immediately this is noticed the accumula-tor should be slowly and thoroughly re-charged, and if the sulphate has not then disappeared it must then be discharged by means of a lamp.

Never short-circuit the terminals with a piece of wire, or the accumulator will be ruined ; a 6-watt motor bulb will do very well. The accumulator should then again be recharged. Now, if the accumulator is kept in a charged state and recharged at regular inter-vals, the sulphation of the plates is not likely to take place. It is usually neglect of this precaution that causes trouble in this respect.

The Electrolyte or Acid

This consists of a weak solution of pure sulphuric acid and distilled water. The correct proportion of acid and water is very important, and

Fig. 4.—REMOVING A TIGHT INSULATED TERMINAL.
In this case a hot iron cannot be used. Therefore, apply a rag dipped in very hot water.

Fig. 5.—Showing
What Happens
to Neglected
Terminals

good service will not be obtained unless the proper proportions are maintained.

One will see on the label of the accumulator the term "Specific gravity of acid." This is the proportion of acid and water, and the correctness of this is found by means of an instrument called a "hydrometer." These simple instruments may be purchased for 1s. or so, and the most suitable type is that in which the hydrometer proper is enclosed in a glass bulb, with a rubber ball

Fig. 6. — Do not use Pliers to Loosen a Stuck Terminal or the Terminal Pillar may be Broken.

at the top and a small rubber tube at the other end. The rubber tube can easily be inserted through the vent of the accumulator by removing the plug, and a small quantity of the acid drawn into the glass bulb so that the density may be checked by the hydrometer.

By means of the hydrometer not only can the condition of the acid be found, but also if the accumulator is in a fully charged condition, as when the accumulator is discharged the gravity of the acid is lower. It is, therefore, most important that, when testing the gravity of the acid, the accumulator is in a fully-charged condition. Actually, the density of the

acid is the only true guide as to whether the accumulator is fully charged.

HOW TO USE THE HYDROMETER

First remove the vent plug which will be found at the top of your accumulator. Next insert through the vent hole the tip of the hydrometer, as shown in Fig. 1. Draw up into the tube a small quantity of accumulator acid and note the reading on the small float inside the tube.

When the battery is fully charged the reading should be 1300. If the battery is only slightly discharged the reading will be about 1250. If the battery is about half discharged the reading will be about 1200. A reading of 1150 would indicate that the battery needed immediate charging.

Fig. 7.—A Sulphated Plate.

White patches on the plates of your battery indicate that it needs immediate attention. The remedy is to recharge and discharge the battery several times until the patches disappear.

It is important to remember that before this test is made the level of acid in the accumulator must be brought up to the level indicated on the case (*see* Fig. 6). This should be done by adding distilled water. A bottle of water for this purpose can be obtained from the local chemist. If only a small quantity is required it is a simple matter to obtain this by using a teapot and kettle to form a rough-and-ready still.

How to Obtain a Small Quantity of Distilled Water at Home

Place a kettle of water on a gas stove and, while it is boiling, rinse out and dry an old teapot. When steam begins to issue from the kettle spout remove the teapot lid, place a wet cloth round the outside of the teapot, and place the teapot over the kettle spout with the teapot spout pointing downwards. In a few seconds drops of distilled water will come from the teapot spout. By wringing out the cloth in cold water occasionally sufficient distilled water could be obtained to top up the accumulator.

It is essential that the acid always covers the top of the plates, and when it falls below this level, due to evaporation, distilled water must be added to cover the plates. Remember that the acid does not evaporate, it is only the water that does so, and this is the reason for only adding distilled water; therefore, unless any acid is lost, due to leakage or excessive spraying in charging, no new acid should be added. It will easily be found if this is necessary, if the gravity of the acid is tested when the accumulator is fully charged. The acid should then read the gravity of that stated on the label of the accumulator, but as a general rule the specific gravity should be 1250-1300.

Some Valuable Hints

Accumulators must be given proper attention if they are to give long service. If a little time is given to looking after the condition, the trouble will be amply repaid. Do not forget that the acid used

in the accumulators is **very dangerous**, and if spilt on such things as **carpets**, clothes, furniture, etc., it will ruin such things in a very short time. If you are unfortunate enough to spill any acid on such articles, immediately cover the place with a strong solution of soda, or, if possible, ammonia. It is always well to keep handy a bottle of strong soda water

Fig. 8.—SPADE TERMINALS SHOULD BE KEPT CLEAN.

A piece of emery cloth is useful for this purpose.

or ammonia in case of any accidents, as an accumulator being knocked over may easily ruin an expensive carpet in a short time; also, often when an accumulator is received from a charging station the bottom is wet with acid; therefore, before standing an accumulator on anything of importance, wipe the bottom with soda or ammonia (soda and ammonia being alkaline substances they will neutralise the acid).

Fig. 9.—A LITTLE VASELINE APPLIED TO THE TERMINALS
OCCASIONALLY WILL PREVENT THE CONDITION SHOWN IN
FIG. 5.

Points to Remember

(1) Add nothing but pure distilled water and do this often enough to keep the plates covered.

(2) Do not over-discharge the accumulator (test the gravity of the acid by means of a hydrometer).

The hydrometer will read 1250 when the cell is fully charged; 1180, half discharged; 1110, fully discharged.

(3) Keep the battery clean, the filling plugs and connections tight.

(4) The terminals smeared with vaseline.

(5) If the cells are in celluloid cases, pour off and discard the old acid once a year, when the accumulator is in a fully-charged condition, and refill with new acid immediately.

AN IMPROVED WASHSTAND

A WOODEN or marble-topped washstand with a ewer and basin is looked upon nowadays as old-fashioned and unsightly. For small bedrooms where some sort of washstand is still a desirable convenience, there is a washstand of new and improved design which, when not in use, has the appearance of a handsome oak dressing-chest. A lift-up top reveals an enamel basin with chain and rubber stopper, and immediately beneath this is a shelf on which stands an enamel pail to receive the used water. There are also an enamel ewer and, on the inner side of the right-hand door, an enamel soap-dish. In the compartment on the left are a shelf and metal shoe-rail. Inside the lift-up top is a frameless mirror.

THE SELECTION AND CARE OF FURS

Fig. 1.—CLEANING FURS.

A good way of cleaning heavy furs like beaver, is to rub them well with hot bran. Afterwards, comb and shake. Only certain furs will stand this, however, and to be on the safe side it is better to send the furs to the furrier for cleaning.

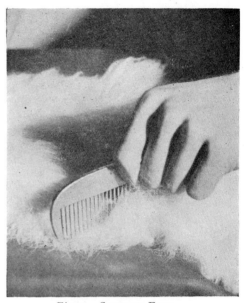

Fig. 2.—COMBING FURS.

Especially if the hair is long, use a metal comb with wide teeth for combing out the fur. An ordinary toilet comb is too fine for this purpose. Comb very gently to avoid dragging out the hairs.

WHEN Mrs. Nanook, of Eskimo Hut, Baffin Land, who moves in the best Arctic circle(s), feels that she needs a new fur coat—or trousers —she acquaints her liege lord, who forthwith, good easy man, sharpens his harpoons, hies him to the icefloes and, having slain a seal or two, drags them home, knowing that, after an enormous banquet on the flesh, the skins, after Mrs. N. has chewed them for many hours, will be converted into the desired garments, also by the efforts of the lady in question, and he will be at peace.

Household Duties for Eskimos

This chewing of skins is one of the Eskimo woman's household duties ; she is the furrier to the family, and her method of reducing the raw skins to a wearable suppleness is to masticate every inch of them for some minutes. She cannot do much in the way of selection. Obviously she must utilise the skins that her husband has succeeded in securing, which renders the more incongruous a remark heard in the British Museum by the writer. A man and woman were gazing attentively at the figure of an Eskimo dressed in seal, and the woman, after a meticulous scrutiny remarked : " She didn't match up the skins very well ! "

A Fur Coat is an Economy

Different women read the word economy in different ways. Considering furs from the hard-wearing point of view, obviously it is not extravagant to spend a little more on a coat that can be relied on to wear for some years, and will be worth

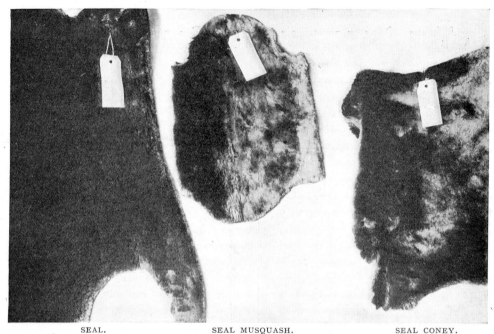

SEAL.   SEAL MUSQUASH.   SEAL CONEY.

Fig. 3.—CAN YOU TELL THESE THREE " SEAL " FURS ?

This shows rabbit and musquash furs treated to imitate the real seal shown on the left.
Seal musquash has to a large extent supplanted the real seal.

Fig. 4.—A SEALSKIN, SPECIALLY TREATED TO SHOW STAGES IN MANUFACTURE.

Right—in natural state, dressed only : centre—top hair removed, exposing light brown
under fur : left—as finally manufactured, machined and dyed seal-brown.

remodelling, rather than to lay out less money on something cheap which will be worn out at the end of a season. On the other hand, a woman who tires rapidly of wearing the same thing, may prefer to buy something inexpensive and renew her purchase when it ceases to be of interest. *Good furs are always worth the money* expended on them, although, at the moment, practically all of them are lower — considerably lower — than they have been for several years.

Of course, if the urge to purchase a chinchilla wrap or a sable coat arises —then furs *are* luxuries, but supposing a woman wishes for something in fur that will look smart, wear well, and not cost too much— what should she look for?

FUR COATS

A good deal depends on the conditions under which the garments are to be worn. Riding in a car, for instance, will wear out a fur coat many times more quickly than merely walking; the more often that one sits down, the quicker will the coat give way.

A natural fur, i.e., one that is not dyed, nor deprived of its top hairs, will last much longer than one in which the reverse is the case; natural musquash,

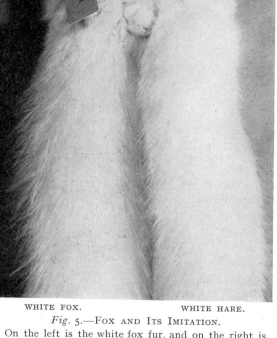

WHITE FOX.   WHITE HARE.
Fig. 5.—Fox and Its Imitation.
On the left is the white fox fur, and on the right is its less expensive imitation.

marten, sable or lynx, for example, wearing better than the dyed varieties of those furs. Against this, however, must be set the fact that most furs sold to the public have, greatly to the benefit of their appearance, made previous acquaintance with the dyer.

Seal, Mink and Astrakan

Formerly, the seal coat offered the best return for one's money; in Victorian days it was like the family plate, produced on great occasions and handed down from mother to daughter for an amazing term of years; and even to-day, although not fashionable, for combined appearance and hardwearing qualities, there is no fur that approaches it, excepting mink, which is decidedly more costly. Next to mink comes Persian lamb or Astrakan, much less expensive, whilst in the Shiraz or half Persian one may obtain something still cheaper, somewhat less effective in appearance and which will wear nearly as well.

Musquash

Coming farther down the scale of durability, one arrives at natural musquash, of which there are three kinds—

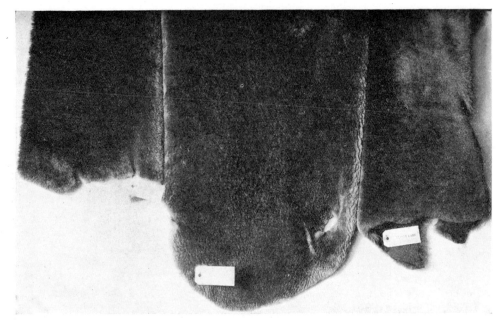

Fig. 6.—ANOTHER PROBLEM FOR THE NON-EXPERT.
Left—nutria ; centre—beaver ; right—beaver lamb. All the same colour and very similar in appearance. The wear is quite another matter.

black (rich and the most expensive), western, and southern ; this last is less heavily furred and can be bought at fairly modest prices.

Nutria and Seal Musquash

From a hard-wearing point of view, nutria appears next, but although one of the standbys of the trade cannot be described as a common or cheap fur, it gains in appearance but loses somewhat in durability from having the top hairs removed. Then comes " Hudson " or seal musquash, a dyed fur, equal to or even better in appearance than seal, but not wearing so well. This fur was originally introduced to imitate seal, and it has now, to all evidence, supplanted it, an important reason being that as it is much softer and easier to work, it is possible to get a much more graceful effect than with seal. Squirrel, a beautiful fur, is rather more delicate and responds to careful handling ; it has dropped steadily in price since October 1927.

Marmot, Mole and Coney

Marmot and its cousin peschanik stand at a very low price to-day, and from a hard-wearing standpoint are on about the same level. Still lower down follow mole and the ubiquitous coney (otherwise rabbit), both sold nowadays at next to no profit for the furrier.

FURS FOR NECKPIECES

The furs so far mentioned are considered from the point of view of coats, but where neckpieces are concerned, hard-wearing furs are otter, bear, raccoon, skunk and wolf, in the order named. Canadian sable or marten wears better than skunk, and baum than stone marten; Australian opossum goes farther than American, and silver fox than lynx; ermine, however, stands harder wear than white fox, but soils easily in cities, and is difficult to get back to its original purity of colour. Kolinsky, in its modern dyes, is a good proposition, inexpensive and of rich appearance. Natural fox comes high on the list, both for appearance and wearing qualities ; it varies amazingly in price, however.

Of trimmings, used so largely on the ever popular cloth or tweed coat, raccoon both looks and wears well; the same remark applies to skunk, whilst for cheapness and hard wear combined one need not look beyond dyed whitecoat, the fur by the way, which, in its natural state is largely used by the Eskimo.

Some Useful Hints on Buying Furs

There are over six hundred fur-bearing animals known to zoologists, and as of

obviously called for. The wisest economy is to go to a *reliable* furrier, state approximately the sum to be expended, and act on his advice. For preference, the furrier should be one who, manufacturing his own goods, can guarantee the authenticity of both the fur and the workmanship.

On no account should furs be purchased from anywhere than from a firm which has a reputation to lose ; the average person's knowledge of furs is nil, and swindles, as old as the three-card trick, and

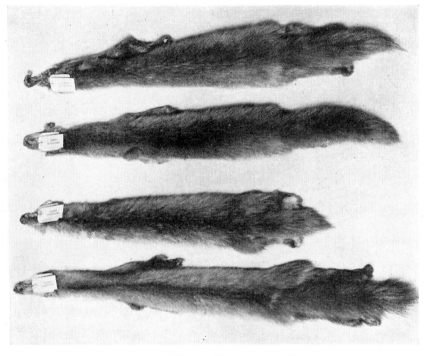

TOPPED
BAUM
MARTEN.

TOPPED
RUSSIAN
SABLE.

NATURAL
RUSSIAN
SABLE.

NATURAL
CANADIAN
SABLE.

Fig. 7.—MARTENS AND SABLES.
Good marten skins are difficult to distinguish from the well-known Russian sable. Canadian sable is marten fur. Badly coloured furs are topped or dyed.

these over one hundred are in common everyday use in the trade, it should be possible to select something to suit the purse of everyone, at the same time not losing sight of such essentials as smartness and durability. Everything depends on the answer to the question : " How much can I afford to spend ? " as when fur coats can be bought from £5 to £5,000, and ties and stoles from 7s. 6d. to £2,000, a certain amount of consideration is

quite as successful, are perpetrated daily on the credulous. The wandering seaman (?) with sables (?) to dispose of, the lady of reduced means who offers her rich furs at ridiculous prices—these should be shunned firmly.

The furs in many specious advertisements are not always what they seem to be.

The Question of Names

Should a store offer furs under such names as " Near-seal," " Sablette," etc., the customer should ask : " What fur is it really ? " The London Fur Trade Association, the controlling body of the trade in Great Britain, lays down that the last word in any description of fur must be that of the animal itself, i.e., beaver *lamb* is a variety of lambskin, mink dyed *musquash* is musquash not mink, etc. There are, however, certain furs which are exceptions to this rule : rabbit, for instance, is known under its Biblical name of coney, and seal-dyed musquash is frequently, particularly in the U.S.A., termed " Hudson."

On the other hand, what the public calls " Seal," is really the sea lion, the true seal being known as hair seal and the young as whitecoat ; the Civet cat is neither a civet nor a cat, but a kind of skunk ; only a small proportion of " Persian " lambs come from Persia ; Galiak may be the young of the Persian lamb, caracul or pony and the Australian kaola is known as wombat.

Guide to the Principal Furs

At this stage the reader may inquire : " How can I tell a fur ? " and the question is extremely difficult to answer. Most fur bearers have two coats :—

(1) The outer, coarse and harsh, known as hair, which protects the inner.

(2) Soft and downy, termed fur.

The furrier frequently removes the hair, thus imparting an entirely different appearance to the skin, e.g., natural musquash, in its natural state a rough long-haired skin of a brown colour is, when dyed and with the hair removed to imitate seal, converted to a short, smooth and velvety pile, almost black in colour.

Some animals, e.g., mole, have no hair, whilst others, such as pony, antelope and calf have no fur. A short guide to some of the more important fur-bearers follows, but it must be realised that cold print is a very imperfect means of describing furs.

BADGER.—Hair grey, tips white, 2 inches to 4 inches long, underfur brown ; length 2 feet to 2 feet 6 inches.

BEAVER.—Hair usually removed. Rich chestnut, underfur nut-brown, about 1 inch long, dark in centre, paler at flanks. Length up to 3 feet.

CHINCHILLA.—The most beautiful of furs, delicate pale grey, dark markings. Length about 18 inches. Two varieties : Peru, fur about 1 inch in length, and Bastard, ½ inch. Very rare, fragile and expensive.

CARACUL.—Smaller than Persian lamb (q.v.), flatter and not tightly curled ; naturally brown in colour, but almost invariably dyed. Good skins are fairly expensive.

ERMINE.—White ; the stoat in his winter dress. In summer he is brown, fur then termed summer ermine. Fur short and close. Length of skin, 10 inches.

FISHER.—Long, practically black hair, fur rich dark brown. The largest of the martens, 2 feet to 3 feet long ; hard-wearing, of good appearance.

FITCH.—Black and yellow or black and cream ; hair long and dark along middle of back, underparts lighter ; hard-wearing and inexpensive.

FOX.—Numerous varieties and colours, the better known being Blue, Cross, Red, Silver and White. Length 2 feet to 2 feet 6 inches ; hair 1 inch to 4 inches.

Blue : Slate colour tinged with brown ; hair rather short. Alaska foxes rather coarser than another species known as Greenland.

Cross : Handsome skin, something between a red and silver fox ; yellow or orange with dark cross marking on shoulders ; usually has silver pointed hairs.

Red : Best are American, large and vividly coloured ; Europeans, with the exception of Norwegians, are inferior. The cheaper sorts are usually dyed black or brown. Price according to quality.

FOX.—Silver, formerly known as " Black." Beautiful skin, with silver hairs, fur black and underfur grey. The skins are graded in accordance with the silvering, which fashion demands shall vary from time to time. Formerly very expensive, is now, owing to the vast numbers raised on farms, reasonably priced.

White or Arctic : Small, only 2 feet in length ; rather more " downy " than red. Unlike other foxes, has no smell.

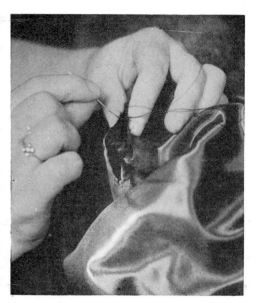

Fig. 8.—REPAIRING A TEAR IN A FUR.
Unstitch the lining and sew the skin at the back like this.   Use a strong needle.

Fig. 9.—REPAIRING A TEAR.
The appearance at the back after sewing quite a big tear.   It is invisible on the front.

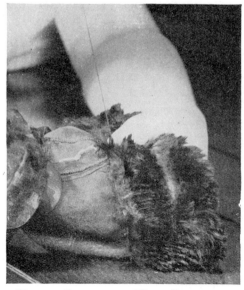

Fig. 10.—TO PUT A PATCH IN A WORN PLACE.
Cut a clean hole, and also a piece of fur the right size.   Sew up the patch as for a tear. This shows the best way to cut fur, from the back, and never with scissors.

Fig. 11.—REPAIRING A WORN CUFF OF A FUR COAT.
Turn the sleeve inside out, untack the lining and turn it back.   Then turn up the cuff to hide the worn place, tack it in place, and re-stitch the lining.

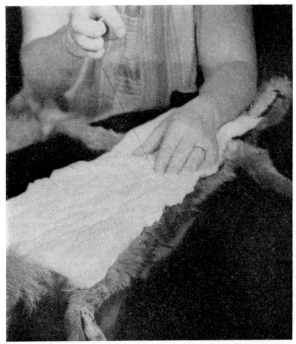

Fig. 12.—To Re-line a Fur—First
Operation.

Remove the old lining and the wadding. Tack on new wadding, and cut
it to shape with scissors.

The cheaper skins are dyed all the
colours of the rainbow in addition
to black.

Hare.—Fragile fur, usually made
up to represent something else,
preferably fox or lynx; white in
winter. Inexpensive.

Kolinsky. — A small Asiatic
marten, sandy-red in colour, and
consequently usually dyed to a
more artistic shade ; quite effective
and inexpensive.

Lamb. — " Persian " lamb or
Astrakan; a curled woolly fur, dyed
an intense black; quality is
evidenced by brilliance and tight-
ness of curl; wears well—and looks
well.

Shiraz or half Persian : As above,
but fur less tightly curled, more
woolly, not so glossy, and less in
price.

Grey Astrakan and *Krimmer* are

naturally grey lambs, the fur
is ringletted ; length up to 18
inches.

Broadtail and *Galyak :* Lambs
with but little fur, such fur being
either a moire pattern, or finer
and flatter than the ordinary
Persian lamb; almost invariably
dyed black ; not a cheap fur.
Many other lambs, dyed and
prepared in a variety of ways,
are to be obtained at a small
cost.

Lynx.—Reddish-brown fur,
with many grey hairs, about 3
inches long; silky and longer
on flanks than on the back ; fur
"flows" freely; frequently dyed
black, when it is superior in
appearance to fox, but is more
fragile ; the skin is about 4 feet
long.

Marmot.—Short rough open
fur, dirty yellow, hair darker,
usually dyed ; length from 1 foot
to 18 inches. Inexpensive.

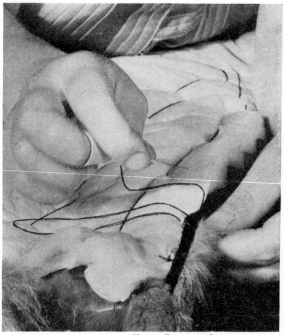

Fig. 13.—Re-lining a Fur—Second Operation.
Then stitch the edge of the wadding all round under
the black binding.

Peschanik and *Suslik* are allied to the Marmot, although smaller ; both are usually dyed, and Peschanik has a sleek appearance, which Marmot has not.

MARTEN.—*Baum* or Pine ; nearly always sold in a dyed condition or topped. Long brown soft fur, with a yellowish throat ; extremely difficult to tell a good skin from Russian Sable. About 2 feet long, with a long full tail.

Stone or Beech : Sold in both natural and dyed conditions ; natural colour is bluish-brown, with white throat and

MINK.—Short, close, thick, somewhat harsh fur of varying shades of brown ; handsome and hardwearing ; tail rather " pokerish."

MOLE.—Very short grey velvety fur, undershade blue. Rather fragile but, being supple, can be worked into very pleasing examples of the furrier's art.

MUSQUASH.—Fur and hair vary a great deal according to the original home of the animal. Brown in colour, underfur bluish-white.

Black Musquash is more heavily furred,

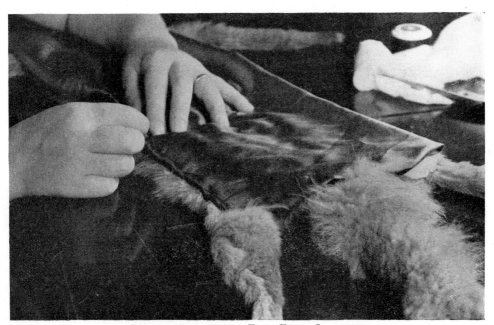

Fig. 14.—RE-LINING A FUR—FINAL OPERATION.
Cut the lining fairly full, turn in the edges and tack in position, and then sew them to the fur.

underfur ; a coarser fur than Baum Marten ; the natural skins are well suited to the blonde type of woman.

Japanese : Smaller, yellow and, therefore, usually dyed ; about 18 inches long. Inexpensive.

American or *Canadian Sable* : A beautiful fur, considered by many as superior in appearance to Russian Sable ; silky, warm brown fur, underfur drab and a dark mark along the spine ; length about 18 inches. Badly coloured skins are topped or dyed ; long full tail.

and the top hairs are much darker.

Southern Musquash is paler and poorer in quality than the others, of which Black is the more expensive. Musquash varies from 6 inches to 12 inches in length.

Dyed : Natural Musquash, unhaired and dyed seal-brown ; resembles seal. Sometimes termed " Hudson."

NUTRIA.—The fur of the Coypu rat ; hair, which is always removed is about 3 inches long ; light brown in colour, and resembles Beaver, but the Nutria fur is much shorter. Skins about 2 feet long.

Fig. 15.—For Replacing Fur Buttons.

Materials required—a circular piece of fur, a button or button mould, wadding, and binding or tape, and some thick cord elastic for the loops.

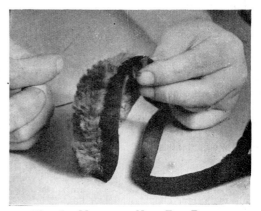

Fig. 16.—Making a New Fur Button.

This shows how to stitch the binding around the bit of fur, tightly so as to begin the shape.

OPOSSUM.—*American :* Fur grey, top hairs a lighter grey and rather sparse, there is a "kink" in this fur which is distinctive ; usually dyed ; length 12 inches to 15 inches.

Australian : Fur clear grey, smoother, shorter and quite different in appearance to American, some skins strongly tinged with red ; length 8 inches to 10 inches.

Tasmanian : Coarser in texture, larger in size than the Australian. Colour a chestnut-brown.

OTTER.—Hair and fur dark nut-brown, short, rich and thick; frequently unhaired. Extremely durable and handsome ; length, European 3 feet, Canadian 3 feet 6 inches. English Otters run smaller.

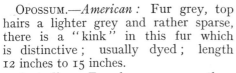

Fig. 17.—Making a New Fur Button— Second Operation.

The button and some wadding above and below it are put in the middle, and the binding is then gathered up.

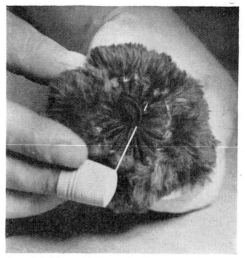

Fig. 18.—New Button Ready to Sew on Coat.

When the binding is nearly gathered, the ends of a short length of elastic are inserted, and the whole is finished with a few strong stitches.

PONY.—Hair only, usually flat and harsh, sometimes shaggy and woolly ; frequently dyed, varies extremely in price.

RABBIT.—Known in trade as *Coney*, is used to imitate all kinds of more expensive furs, never seen as a fur in its natural state.

RACCOON.—Hairs black and white, fur long and greyish-brown, underfur thick and very dark ; has a ringed tail ; length of skin from 2 feet 6 inches to 3 feet.

SABLE.—Resembles American Marten, only darker and not so warm in colour, soft, silky and long-haired ; many skins have silver hairs amongst the dark ; cheaper skins topped or dyed ; beautiful and expensive.

SEAL (Fur).—Probably coming into vogue again as, owing to careful conservation, the herds have enormously increased of late years. Never sold in its natural form, but always unhaired and dyed a rich dark brown. Short close thick fur, soft and velvety ; length 2 feet to 3 feet.

SEAL (Hair).—The true seal, close bristly hair, no fur. Yellowish-grey, with dark round marks. Too thick in leather for women's wear. The young, known as Whitecoats are softer and more pliable ; usually dyed and used as trimmings.

SKUNK.—Dark brown fur, with white markings, slightly rough and long ; hard-wearing and solid ; size of a cat. The South American variety is smaller, lighter in colour, silkier, and does not wear so well.

SQUIRREL.—Fur, grey on back, white on belly ; usually backs only utilised ; soft, pretty and popular.

WALLABY.—Red-brown, sometimes hair only, from 1 inch to 3 inches in length ; rather coarse, usually dyed. Inexpensive.

How to Detect a Dyed Skin

Many furs are topped—i.e., they have the top hairs lightly brushed with dye to give them a richer colouring than they naturally possess. When skilfully done, this process greatly improves the look of the skin and it is very difficult to discern. One can usually detect a dyed skin by blowing the fur apart and looking at the leather, when the dye may be perceived. The *carefully* sewn seams, to be

found in every fur garment do not mean weakness, for the cutter's knife is used on, one may say, every skin that is made up, greatly improving its appearance, it may be added.

It is well to be on one's guard against imitations ; in no trade are there as many cheap articles having the appearance of expensive ones as in the fur trade, and *only an expert can tell them.*

CARE OF FURS

Furs are worth taking care of, and a little thought, translated into action will ensure their keeping fresh for a long time.

How and Where to Hang Them

First and foremost keep your furs hanging up—if a coat, on a shoulder or hanger, which, preferably, should be padded ; if a stole, from a hook, head uppermost, so that the hair " flows " naturally, and keep them in darkness. The rays of the sun have a very bad effect on furs, reducing their colour and sheen to a marked degree.

Do Not Finger Them

When taking them down and handling them, touch the fur as little as possible, first because friction soon breaks away the top hairs, and, second, because the human hand is always—dreadful as it may sound—slightly moist, slightly greasy and slightly acid, and moisture, grease and acid are no friends to manufactured furs. Shake the garments before putting them on and after taking them off ; shake them as the fur " flows "— i.e., from the head and not the tail end.

Periodical Attention

Examine them carefully for any " matting " or entangling and carefully comb out such, using a metal comb, with teeth set not too closely. Occasionally, if you love them, beat them with a light cane, but always put them on a cushion, well filled for preference, and not on a bare table. After beating, comb carefully.

Fighting Moth

The tighter your wardrobe door fits the less risk of moth. The moths that are so destructive to furs are the small variety with us during most of the year, and not the big blundering species. They lay their eggs at the base of the hairs and, when in due course the grubs hatch out, they feed on the roots, causing the hairs to fall out ; bare patches ensue, the fur gets matted and sticky and, unless matters are arrested, the fur is ruined. Beating and combing are the best preventatives for furs kept at home, but the really sound thing is to send them to cold storage, where the dry cold air, although fatal to moths, has a wonderfully reviving effect on the furs themselves. By the way, moths do not like dyed furs.

If moth *does* get into your furs send them to a furrier's without delay.

If Furs Get Wet

If your furs get wet *never* dry them at a fire—hang them up. Let them dry gradually, in a draught for preference and, after the moisture has evaporated, shake and comb. It may be necessary to repeat the operation.

Cleaning

When furs get greasy and dirty send them to the furrier ; to attempt to clean valuable furs at home, whilst amusing is apt to be expensive, and when they show signs of wear, do not delay in letting your furrier see them ; hesitation may cost you pounds. One other hint : get your repairs and alterations done in early spring and buy your new furs before autumn. The fashions for the following winter will have been decided on months previously ; you will get the cream of the stock and the salespeople can give that extra attention that, perforce, they will be unable to in the rush of the season.

AN IMPROVED SERVICE WAGON

A NEW "ATCRAFT" TEA TROLLEY WHICH IS CONVERTIBLE FOR USE AS TWO OCCASIONAL TABLES.

A SERVICE wagon on which dishes, food and cutlery may be wheeled to and fro between kitchen and dining-room is a great advantage. It saves an immense amount of time and energy, because everything required for a meal can be taken from one room to the other in one journey. Without a wagon it would be necessary to pass to and fro several times, and in the course of a year a wagon therefore saves you literally miles of walking.

The example illustrated is an improvement on the ordinary kind of service wagon, because the top half is made to lift off. When the wagon is not being used, you thus have the advantage of a pair of occasional tables. Suppose, for example, afternoon tea were being wheeled into the sitting-room when one or two visitors were present, on converting this " Atcraft " wagon you would have two useful tea tables. In wagon form the feet of the upper table fit nicely into sockets, so that it is quite firm and reliable.

Removing a Glass Stopper

WHICH HAS BECOME FIXED

Fig. 1.—Using Warm Water.

to and fro. The friction will warm and so expand the neck before the heat penetrates to the stopper. By this method a more intense local heat can be applied just where it is required. In this case, however, the heat melts the tiny crystals of salt which may be responsible for the binding action.

Mechanical Force

This method is often effective by itself, but is easier if one of the previous operations has been done first. Grasp the bottle as shown, with the thumb pressing hard against the stopper with an upward tendency. Then tap briskly, but not too hard, on the opposite side of the stopper with some *wooden* object. Extreme care should be used as it is very easy to snap the neck of the stopper.

Using Warm Water

TO remove a glass stopper which has stuck, a good way is to place the bottle in a jug of warm water. The water

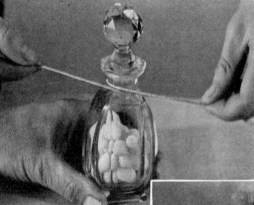

Fig. 2.—Using Friction.

should not be too hot to start with, but hotter water may be used once the bottle has got warmed right through.

The bottle should be kept in the water nearly up to the neck. Heat causes the glass to expand slightly, and in most cases it will be found that this expansion of the neck is sufficient to free the stopper.

Using a Piece of String

Another way of loosening a stuck stopper is to loop a piece of string round the neck of the bottle. Getting someone to hold the bottle firmly, work the string

Fig. 3.—This method must be used with discretion. *See* Text.

Plain Needlework Stitches

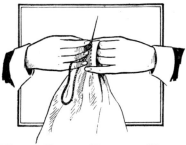

Fig. 1.—How to Hold the Work.

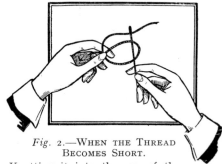

Fig. 2.—When the Thread
Becomes Short.

When sewing without a cushion, hold the material between the thumb and forefinger. By working always towards you, it is a simple matter to keep the stitches straight and even. For fine work a thread should be drawn or a tacking thread used.

Knotting it into the eye of the needle as shown, may enable you to finish the work without threading a fresh supply. This should only be done when sufficiently close to the end of the sewing.

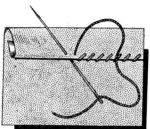

Fig. 3.—Plain Hem.

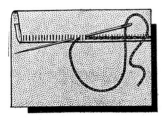

Fig. 4.—A Stitched Hem.

Insert the needle and secure the thread just under the edge of the fold. Direct the needle at a slant to the left. Make a series of regular stitches as shown. Care should be taken when finishing a length of thread to avoid a knot. The new thread should be tucked up under the hem and worked along.

Make a double turning as above, and stitch through the three layers. This shows the right side of the work. Note the method of stitching. Care should be taken to put the needle in again at the same point where it was drawn out on the previous stitch.

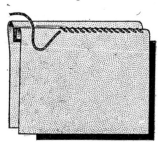

Fig. 5.—Hemming Double Seams.

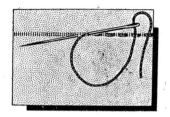

Fig. 6.—Back-Stitching.

Turn in the two raw edges and lay them one upon the other, so that the one next the forefinger lies slightly higher than the one next the thumb. Insert the needle first into the upper edge and then, slightly slanting into the lower one. This stitch is useful for fastening down linings.

Take up six threads of the material. Then insert the needle three threads back from where it was last drawn out, and bring it through again six threads beyond. The appearance of the back-stitch depends on the accuracy of the spacing.

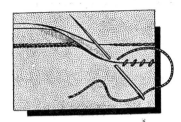

Fig. 7.—MAKING A FLAT SEAM.

Lay the two edges together. Tack together with stitches ¾ inch from the edge. Then back-stitch, following the tacking thread. Trim the inner edge, turn down the outer one and fell it down. Smooth down under edge as you proceed.

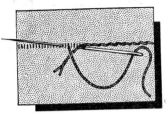

Fig. 8.—SEAMING.

Avoiding knots in back-stitching and running by winding the old thread with the new until used up.

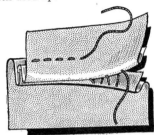

Fig. 10.—THE DOUBLE OR FRENCH SEAM.

Used for joining materials liable to fray at the edge. Run the two pieces of material together back to back, perfectly even, turn over close to seam with raw edges enclosed and run together again. Fig. 11 shows another view of the same stitch.

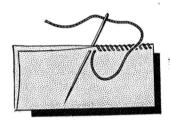

Fig. 9.—JOINING SELVEDGES.

Shows a top- or over-sewing stitch. Tack or pin the materials together before starting to work. Set stitches not more than two or three threads apart.

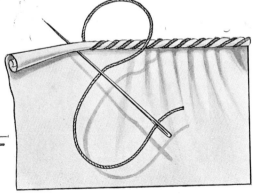

Fig. 12.—WHIPPING.

A form of gathering used for fine materials. With the thumb and forefinger of the left hand, roll the edge over into a very tight, thin roll, little by little, inserting the needle inside the roll next the thumb, bring it out on the outside next the forefinger. Stitch at regular intervals. Draw up the thread as in running, after having taken several stitches. Gathers will form naturally on tightening the draw thread.

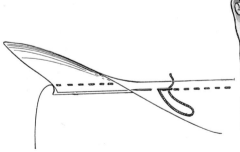

Fig. 11.—DOUBLE OR FRENCH SEAM.

Another view of the same stitch as the one shown in Fig. 10. The neat appearance this method gives to the work is shown to better advantage in this picture. This seam is considerably used for delicate fabrics, such as muslin, crêpe-de-Chine and lace, as well as for dresses that are meant to stand hard wear.

CUTTING MATERIALS STRAIGHT

LINEN, ARTIFICIAL SILK AND COTTON GOODS

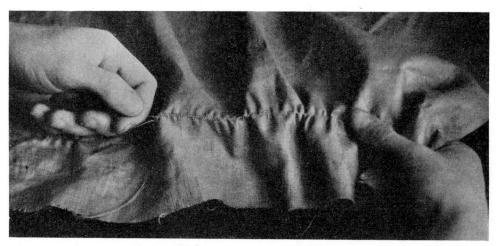

Fig. 1.—For materials such as linen, and some artificial silks, pick up a thread with a pin, and draw it while gathering the material on it. When the whole thread is drawn out, it will leave a clearly visible line as a guide for cutting with the scissors. With some materials, better results are obtained by a sharp tear (*see* Figs. 2 and 3 below).

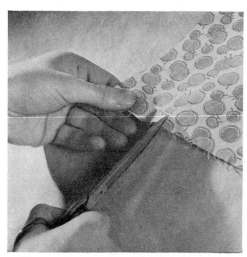

Fig. 2.—CALICO, GINGHAM AND COTTON GOODS.

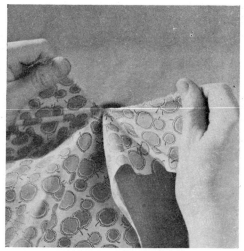

Fig. 3.—CALICO, GINGHAM AND COTTON GOODS.

First make a small snip at one edge as shown above. The snip must, of course, be made where the material is to be parted.

The material can now be torn across cleanly as shown above. This method is specially suited for calico, gingham and cotton goods.

SHELVES IN THE HOME

USEFUL IDEAS BY A PRACTICAL MAN

ALTHOUGH the majority of shelves are utilitarian, there are occasions when they can be made to form a definite part of the decorative scheme of a room. In any case, it is well worth while considering a few methods of treatment in order to arrive at what will best harmonise with the surroundings. Such considerations, of course, are in addition to those of suitability of purpose for which they are required.

Shelves in Recesses

The simplest shelves are those fitted in a recess. The recess itself seems to suggest the addition of shelves, for the side supports are easily fitted to the walls. Fig. 7 shows such an arrangement for shelves at the side of the chimney-breast. The lower cupboard fitment is often already provided in the house and, since it is impossible to stand a piece of furniture in the recess, it seems an excellent use of the space. The kind of

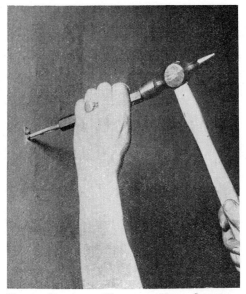

Fig. 1.—PLUGGING WALLS TO HOLD SHELVES. Making the hole for the rawlplug in plaster with a " bullet " tool.

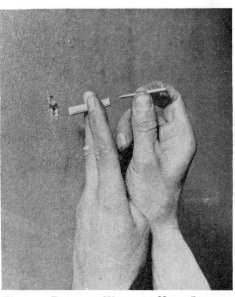

Fig. 1A.—PLUGGING WALLS TO HOLD SHELVES. Close-up view of the rawlplug and screw.

shelves used and the material for them depends upon the purpose for which they are required. As a rule they are to hold books, and this calls for fairly substantial material, since books are heavy. A suitable thickness is $\frac{7}{8}$ inch. A depth of 7 inches is ample for the average books found in the household.

To provide support at the ends the usual method is to fix battens to the walls. These can be of the same thickness as the shelves themselves, with a width of $1\frac{1}{2}$ to 2 inches. A neat finish is given by rounding over the front ends. This is shown clearly in Fig. 2, which also gives a method of ensuring that the shelves are level. A plain strip of wood is held under the batten while the nails are being driven in; it is then taken to the other side as a guide.

The uprights beneath the top shelf and the shaped pieces in the side compartments, form an interesting

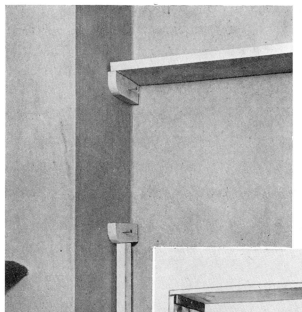

in Fig. 7), it is desirable to fix a thin strip of wood near the back to prevent the plates from slipping forward. This method certainly has the advantage of simplicity, though those who have the facilities may prefer to run a groove along instead.

Shelves with Wooden Uprights

It will be appreciated that it is not always desirable to fix battens to the wall. In some cases it may not be practicable, possibly owing to the fragile nature of the wall

*Fig. 2.—*PUTTING UP SHELVES IN A RECESS.

Note the neat finish given to the battens on the wall by rounding them in front. To ensure that the shelves are fitted level, hold a strip of wood under the batten while the nails are being driven in. The completed shelves are shown in Fig. 7.

addition. If these are to be adopted they should be fixed between the shelves, and the whole thing fixed in position as a complete unit. The niches so formed provide convenient standing space for ornaments.

When certain of the shelves are intended to hold plates (*see* top shelf

*Fig. 3.—*BOOKSHELVES WITH WOODEN UPRIGHTS.
This saves the necessity of fixing supporting battens to the wall.

itself. This necessitates the provision of wooden uprights to which the shelves can be fixed.

Fig. 3 gives an example. The two main uprights are marked out with the positions of the shelves, and the battens are nailed at these lines without difficulty. It is obvious that the centre upright, if required,

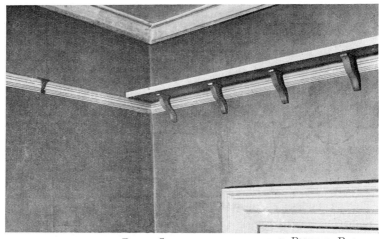

Fig. 4.—ATTRACTIVE PLATE SHELF FIXED ABOVE THE PICTURE RAIL.

cannot be in one piece. This means that a series of short lengths have to be fitted between. A simple method of fixing them is to drive in the nails askew. Every shelf of 30 inches or more in length should have this additional support at the centre if it has to support a heavy weight.

The Picture Rail Shelf

An example of a shelf whose decorative properties are equal to those of utility is shown in Fig. 4. It is fixed above the picture rail and is suitable for plates and other light objects. Nails are used to fix it down on to the rail, and a series of shaped brackets is fixed to the underside to provide the necessary support at the front.

The small brackets are about ¾ inch thick, and are so shaped that they clear the picture rail itself, although they touch both the shelf and the wall. Fig. 5 gives the method of assembling. Note how a square is held at the back edge of the shelf as a guide to keeping the edges of the brackets in line. It is desirable to provide a strip of wood a short distance from the back edge at the top to prevent the plates from slipping forward.

Fig. 8 shows a handy form of rack suitable for the living-room. It is made up as a complete unit and is fixed to the wall with metal plates. As the shelves are extra narrow, cross strips are screwed to the uprights to prevent accidents in the event of the plates falling forward. Such

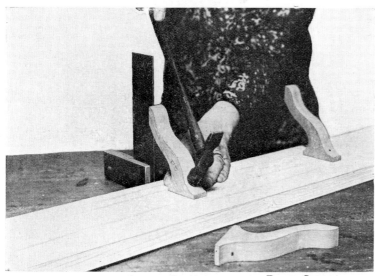

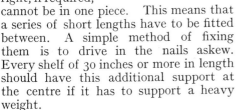

Fig. 5.—FIXING SHAPED BRACKETS TO THE PLATE SHELF.

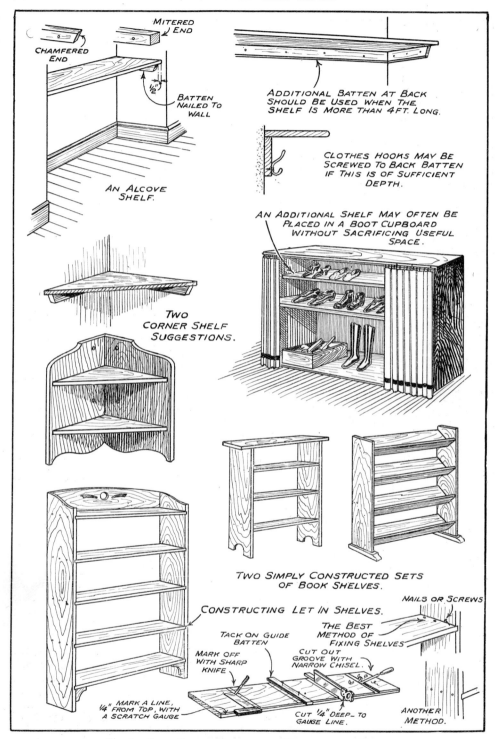

Fig. 6.—SOME SIMPLE SHELVES TO MAKE IN THE HOME.

Fig. 7.—BOOKSHELVES BUILT INTO A RECESS.
The lower cupboard is often already provided in the house on each side of the chimneybreast, and the space above it is excellent for the purpose illustrated. The shelves can be made to provide variety of decoration in the room.

shelves have considerable decorative value, especially if made in oak.

Some Simple Shelves to Make

Fig. 6 shows some simple suggestions for constructing shelves, including alcove, boot cupboard, corner and bookshelves. The most important point to note is the method by which the shelves are supported. It will be seen that some are supported by battens at the ends of the shelves. The simplest method of fixing the shelf is by nails or screws driven into the side pieces, and is shown in the case of two of the bookshelves. It is not a method to be favoured, because the fixing lacks strength. Nailed or screwed shelves of trough form, as shown, may be made by this method with the assurance of sufficient strength for ordinary bookshelf use. The best method of constructing bookshelves is by letting the shelf some $\frac{1}{4}$ inch into the side pieces, and then inserting nails or screws.

Plugging Walls to Hold Shelves

A convenient way of plugging a wall to hold shelves is to use rawlplugs. These consist of a fibrous tube which fits in a hole made in the wall. When the screw is driven in the fibre expands and grips tightly in its hole. Special outfits containing various sizes of plugs, screws and tools are obtainable.

The choice of tool is important. For a brick, concrete, or similar wall the fluted tool is used ; for plaster the "bullet" tool, which is smooth, is the better. Fig. 1 shows the tool being used. It should not be driven in like a nail, but should be turned after each blow with the hammer to prevent it from becoming wedged. It is important that the correct size of screw is used for the particular rawlplug.

Fig. 8.—USEFUL PLATE SHELVES FIXED AS A WHOLE TO THE WALL.

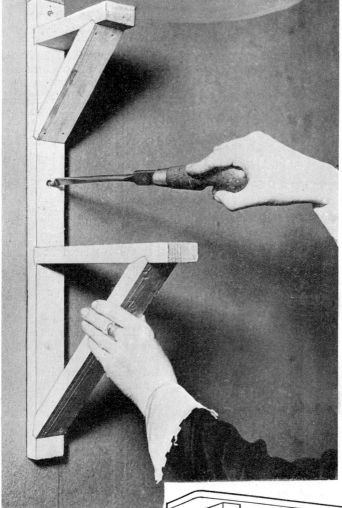

advisable to call in the aid of a carpenter to make the brackets, because the diagonal pieces have to be notched into the others to give the necessary strength.

Fig. 9 shows one of the brackets being screwed to the wall. It is generally necessary to use rawlplugs in the wall to enable the screws to grip properly.

Glass Shelves

These are coming in for increasing use in the bathroom. They have the advantage of being easily cleaned and are light. Special plate-glass shelves with rounded edges can be obtained; also proper nickelled brackets to support them.

Fig. 11 shows the method of attachment to the wall. It is advisable to use nickelled screws, as these are not likely to rust in the damp atmosphere of the bathroom. Where

Fig. 9.—Screwing Shelf Brackets to the Wall.

Similarly, the right size tool must be chosen. Fig. 1A shows the rawlplug with its screw.

Scullery Shelves

As a rule, scullery shelves have to be substantial because they sustain a fair weight and are in constant use. Fig. 10 shows a thoroughly strong set of two shelves. The whole thing is made in wood throughout. It may be

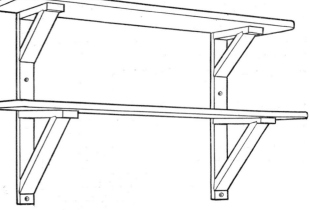

Fig. 10.—Strong Scullery Shelves with Wooden Brackets.

a wooden wall is available there is no difficulty in fixing, for the screws can be driven straight in. It is not practicable to do this in a brick or other wall except by the use of rawlplugs. A good plan is to screw the brackets to a piece of wood, the same length as the shelf, using screw and rawlplugs to fix to the wall.

Corner Shelves

A handy fitment suitable for a corner is shown in Fig. 12. Although the whole thing is made up complete in itself, it is desirable to fix battens to the walls to support the shelves. Whether the lower cupboard accommodation is provided is a matter the reader can decide personally. It could be

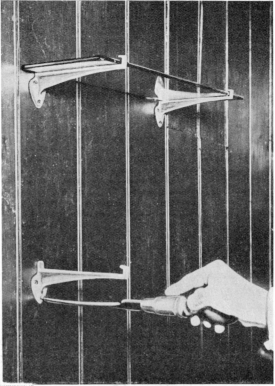

Fig. 11.—GLASS SHELVES FOR THE BATHROOM FIXED WITH METAL BRACKETS.

carried out quite cheaply in deal painted or stained to match the other woodwork in the room.

Lath and Plaster Walls

Where shelves have to be fixed to a lath and plaster wall the nails must be driven into the vertical uprights. The position of these uprights can be found by examining the skirting board. Nails will be seen where the skirting board is fixed to the uprights, and it will be quite safe to fix the shelf supports in a vertical line above these nails. A simple method is to use a weighted string as a guide to find the points vertically above the nails in the skirting board.

Fig. 12.—CORNER FITMENT INCORPORATING USEFUL SHELVES.

SIMPLE DECORATIVE DYEING

*Fig. 1.—*Much Simpler than it Looks.

A nightdress or pyjama case, with a rose ornamentation, is shown on the right. The rose
is made from strips of pink-dyed organdie, shown on the left.

THERE are innumerable useful articles that may be made up from dyed fabrics, but to be successful it is advisable to obtain some experience in the simpler forms of dyeing.

Begin with Simple Effects

To begin with, it is best to experiment with one particular colour and vary the depths of tone that may be obtained. There are many prepared dyes obtainable, some being easier to manipulate than others, but there is really very little difference between any of the advertised brands of dye.

The experience gained by a thorough knowledge of the processes required in dealing with one colour will render it much easier to deal with other colours and will enable the worker to undertake much more ambitious effects. Beautiful effects, brought about by the combination of contrasting and harmonious colourings, can only be obtained by an appreciation of colour harmony.

In this article dyeing in its simplest form will be described. The POPULAR HOME BOOK will contain several other articles dealing with decorative dyeing in all its branches. Providing that ordinary care is taken and the best materials are used, successful results are bound to follow.

A Nightdress Case

An attractive piece of work suitable for the beginner is shown in Fig. 1. This is a nightdress or pyjama case. A large rose ornamentation is sewn to the case, which is padded to make it appear full. The rose is in five shades of pink, with a bunch of stamens in the centre.

Materials Required

The material used for the decoration is white organdie. Either silk or sateen can be used for the bag. 1 yard of organdie 44 inches wide will be found sufficient ; also required is a small enamel bowl, a small basin, a larger bowl for rinsing, a stirring stick and a Fairy dye in rose-pink colour.

The organdie should be torn into strips the width of the material. It tears as easily as calico, and in the same way. Five pairs of strips should be torn, each pair being 4 inches, 3½ inches, 3 inches, 2½ inches, and 2 inches wide.

Dyeing the Strips of Organdie

Mix half a packet of the dye in a small basin with boiling water. Great care must be taken to see that no particles are left. Add the mixture to sufficient cold water to make up a quart.

Now thoroughly wet the organdie, wring it out and place it on one side so that it does not get splashed. Take the two 4-inch pieces and lower them gently into the dye bath. They should be thoroughly stirred about with the stick while the liquid is gradually brought up to the boil. By then the two strips should be the colour desired. Remember to dye the material rather deeper than required, as in rinsing and drying it becomes several shades lighter. It is a good plan to have a few scraps of material for testing. When the colour is right, move the bowl away from the gas ring, take the muslin out, place in the rinsing bowl and rinse thoroughly in several fresh supplies of water until the water fails to remove any more dye.

Now put another ¾ of a pint of cold water in the bowl and replace over the gas ring, add the next two lengths of organdie, that is the 3½-inch width. Repeat the process as before. Do the same with each pair of widths until the five shades have been completed. Always remember to add the cold water between each process in order to make the difference in the shading.

Dry the Dyed Strips

The dyed strips should now be hung up, preferably in the house, as pegging out should be avoided. When nearly dry, iron the strips with a fairly warm iron, placing them under an old piece of soft sheeting.

Making up the Bag

Making up the bag will present no difficulty to the needlewoman. The material should be in a shade of rose-pink to harmonise. One yard will be sufficient if sateen is used, that is if it is 30 inches wide. Four pieces 15 inches square are required. If silk is used, 1¾ yard will be needed, as silk is narrower and would cut

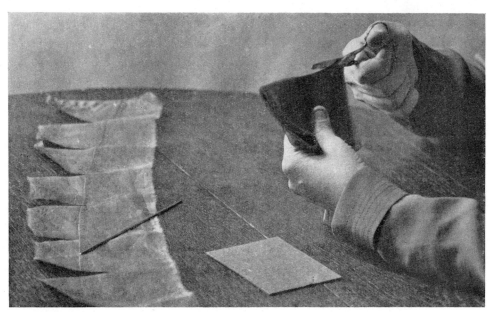

Fig. 2.—CUTTING THE FOLDED MATERIAL TO FORM THE PETALS.
Note the piece of cardboard on which the muslin strip is wound before cutting. When cut, the material will appear as seen on the left.

Fig. 3.—FORMING THE CURL ON THE PETALS.
Roll the corners of the muslin round a large knitting needle.

to waste. Silk adds more to the beauty of the case when finished. In addition, 1 yard of wadding is required for the padding.

After cutting the four pieces 15 inches square, cut the corners round. Then make up the two pads, cutting the wadding to the size, and use it as a filling for each pad.

The Rose Design

Now that the case is ready the rose can be proceeded with; the work is much simpler to make than it looks, and when finished it is so charming it well repays a little patience in preparing the petals.

Making the Petals

The two pieces of dark organdie are for the outer edge. Cut 9 inches off one strip. Cut a piece of fairly stiff cardboard 3 inches wide and 4 inches long. Then wind the muslin round and round the width of the cardboard. When all of it is wound round slip it off the card. Trim one end to make perfectly tidy, and then cut down half-way either side to form the petals, as shown in Fig. 2.

Shaping the Petals

Now roll one corner of the petal round a large knitting needle as seen in Fig. 3.

Hold the needle quite tightly between the first finger and thumb of both hands. Then pull the needle out sharply. The other side of the petal is rolled in the opposite direction, thus forming a triangular end. Continue this procedure until all the cut petals have been shaped. Turn the other side up $\frac{1}{8}$ inch, and gather all along. The piece should not be joined; it will fall in quite naturally as it is being sewn on.

The prepared strip should be placed on the pad, allowing it to lap over $1\frac{1}{2}$ inch at the outer rim. Pin it top and bottom and each side first, to get it even, then sew it on firmly all round.

Preparing the Other Petals

The length of the second strip should be reduced by 18 inches, and wound round the same piece of cardboard, removing and cutting, trimming and curling it similarly to the first strip. In attaching it to the foundation, place it $1\frac{1}{2}$ inch nearer the centre, and arrange the tips of the petals as far as possible in between those of the outer round.

In dealing with the third row the procedure is quite similar, but the strips should be wound on a piece of cardboard measuring only $2\frac{1}{2}$ inches, and the length reduced ¾ yard. The fourth row is reduced still more, cutting off 1 yard altogether. The two centre rows, which are composed of the same tint, are wound on a 2-inch strip of cardboard, and are the same length as the fourth strip. In each case care should be taken to form a close curl, and to arrange the points to alternate with those below.

Stamens

To complete the flower effect sew on a bunch of stamens in black or gold as preferred. These are obtainable in bundles in several lengths. Tie one or two bundles together (according to the size desired) very tightly in the centre. The stamens are now spread out evenly, taking care that the centre does not separate. To finish off the case the lower pad is sewn to the upper one, leaving an opening for the night apparel to be placed inside.

Using Up Left-Over Material

Many opportunities may be found for using up the short lengths of the dyed material left over. One suggestion is to use them to make a small decorative rose with the lightest colour outside and the dark in the centre, as it will be noted there is less of the dark shade left than the light. Attached to a smaller case made of silk or sateen in a similar manner to that described above, it would make a charming little handkerchief sachet.

Another method of using the strips would be to dress a doll for a telephone cover for the bedroom. Still another suggestion is to make the strips up as a rose on a foundation of some stiff material (linenette would do). This could be attached with seccotine to the top of a round chocolate box, and instead of the stamen centre, a handle can be formed with a doll's head, or a pretty decorative button.

CLEANING INSIDE GLASS VESSELS

A USEFUL TIP FOR CLEANING VASES AND LAMP GLASSES

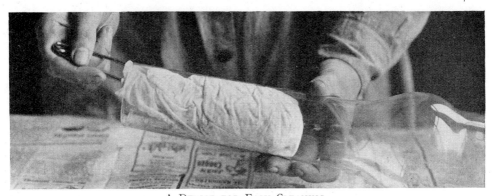

A DEVICE FOR EASY CLEANING.
Expanding wire clip used for cleaning inside lamp glasses and other things.

LAMP glasses, vases, and other articles of a similar form, can easily be cleaned and polished on the inside with the aid of the device shown in the photograph. It consists of a piece of springy wire coiled in the middle of its length, so that the two ends expand. Thus, when it is inserted into a duster, the latter is pressed firmly against the glass and can be easily rotated inside.

New Shoes For Old

IT is disappointing to find that a favourite pair of dress shoes, quite sound in sole and heel, have become unsuitable for wear with a dainty dress. With shoes of velvet or satin, the toes often become so badly rubbed as to be unsightly ; shoes of silver or gold tinsel lose their attractiveness when the tinsel has tarnished.

It is possible to do something with such dilapidated footwear, as Fig. 1 shows. The example illustrated is a pair of silver tinsel shoes, badly tarnished, but otherwise in good condition. The transformation is brought about by using embroidery silks in four shades of turquoise-blue. Expert needlecraft is not required ; the method is quite simple, a little time and patience only being needed.

Making the "Uppers" look like New

As will be seen in the illustration, the embroidery silks are lightly darned all over the shoe, the darkest shade being placed at the toe, which is generally the most soiled portion. During the process of darning, just a few only of the silver threads underneath should be taken up; no more than is necessary to keep the silks in position. Actually, the original but tarnished silver tinsel forms a background, and tends to impart a very pleasing effect to the colours above.

Balancing the Colours

Some care must be taken in working out the colours to obtain a good balance or graduation of shades, and special attention should be paid to make the pattern approximately the same on both shoes. If this is neglected, the effect is liable to appear amateurish. Black shoes look particularly well treated in this way, as the background shows up the colour most effectively. A little gold or silver thread introduced is quite a good plan and will add considerably to the brilliancy of the pattern.

Renovating the Heels

To complete the shoes, it will be necessary to treat the heels in some way. They may be lacquered, or in some cases an application of stain will do, particularly if the heels are fabric covered. It is better to leave the lacquering or staining until after the darning is done, owing to the large amount of handling that is necessary, but it may be done first, providing sufficient time is left for it to dry. There is little risk, however, of damaging the newly darned work if a piece of cardboard is placed at the junction of the heel with the upper.

*Fig. 1.—*A New Way of Renovating Old Shoes.
By darning embroidery silks, such as " Star Sylko," all over the " uppers."

STAINING SHOES

Leather shoes which have become shabby can be stained a darker colour by using " Diamine " stain. About one bottle of stain is required for each pair of shoes. Fig. 2 shows how the stain is applied to the shoes. First of all the leather or other fabric should be washed with soap and warm water. Then rinsed thoroughly. The shoes must then be stuffed with paper and put on one side to dry. Particular care must be taken not to handle the washed surface as any grease would prevent proper application of the stain.

Applying the Stain

Using the pad which is attached to the cork, apply the stain to the shoe, beginning round the welt with a straight movement. Force the pad well into the crevice between the welt and the upper.

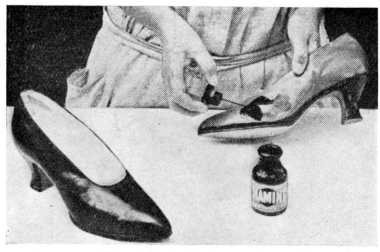

Fig. 2.—STAINING A LEATHER SHOE.
Notice that the welt and heel have been completed first and that the stain is now being applied with a quick circular motion to the upper.

Next stain the heel and then, using a circular movement, rub the stain all over the surface of the upper. It is important to work as quickly as possible and to finish the whole shoe before the stain has dried. This will avoid patches. The best result is obtained by applying two or three coats. In this way any slight unevenness in each coat is smoothed out. If this method is used the first coat must be allowed to dry before the second is applied.

Polishing

After a leather shoe has been stained it should be polished preferably with a cream polish.

STAINING FABRIC SHOES

Fabric shoes may be stained in the same manner, and it will be found that most fabrics take the stain more easily than leather, so that only one coat is usually necessary.

It may be mentioned that leather belts and handbags that have become shabby or stained can often be given a new lease of life if they are stained in the manner described above. With leather articles it is important to apply the stain quickly so as to get the whole surface covered before the stain has had time to dry.

Fig. 3.—A beige coloured shoe which has become shabby can easily be renovated by using a suitable leather stain.

WE have chosen chairs to exemplify our subject because they, above all other kinds of furniture, show the progress of style. The general form of the chair cannot be altered fundamentally. It varies in detail in accordance with the skill of the craftsman, the material available, and the dictates of fashion, and it is preci these points that are so useful when dating a piece of furnit Later in this work are given plates dealing with the chief per such as Tudor, Jacobean, Queen Anne in greater detail.

The Oak Period

OAK CHAIR. About 1525. A heavy type of chair panelled throughout. Mortise and tenon joints are used, pegs being used to secure them. Sometimes panels are carved with linenfold or medallion devices.

OAK CHAIR. Late sixteenth century. A direct descendant from the chair to the left. It has been lightened by the omission of the panelling beneath the seat. The capping above the back is typical.

UPHOLSTERED CHAIR. Early sev teenth century. This is of special intere as it is the earliest form of upholstered ch in England. Crimson velvet was the us covering, with fringes of silk and gold.

The Walnut Period

WALNUT CHAIR. About 1675. A typical Charles II chair. Early walnut work followed on somewhat similar lines to that of the preceding oak period, though it was lighter. The cherub's head and crown were frequently used in the carving.

OAK CHAIR. Late seventeenth century. This is included here because, although of oak, it shows a definite transitional period in its form. The lower seat part is still characteristically "oak," but the back foreshadows the coming style.

WALNUT CHAIR. Early eighteer century. The zenith of the walnut peri The stretcher rails have disappeared entire and the square back has become elaborat shaped, as foreshadowed to the left. T cabriole legs should be noted.

56

he following are the approximate dates covered by the Periods

Styles :—					
OR GOTHIC	..	..	..	..	1485–1558.
ZABETHAN	..	..	..	..	1558–1603.
OBEAN	..	..	..	..	1603–1649.
MWELLIAN	..	..	..	..	1649–1660.

JACOBEAN	..	..	..	..	1660–1688.
WILLIAM AND MARY	..	..	..	..	1689–1702.
QUEEN ANNE	..	..	..	..	1702–1714.
GEORGIAN	..	..	..	..	1714–1749.
CHIPPENDALE	..	..	..	..	1750–1779.
HEPPLEWHITE, ADAM, SHERATON	..	..	1760–1820.

The Mahogany Period

HOGANY CHAIR. Mid-eighteenth tury. A popular form of Chippendale ir. The shape of the back and the rced slat are definitely characteristic.

MAHOGANY CHAIR. Second half eighteenth century. Note that the cabriole leg has been superseded by the lighter tapered type. The shape of the arms is characteristic.

MAHOGANY CHAIR. Second half eighteenth century. Hepplewhite, who evolved this form, became one of the leading stylists. The shield back was a favourite *motif*. A variation is the oval back.

The Satinwood Period

AHOGANY CHAIR. Second half hteenth century. Although of mahogany. s chair belongs to the satinwood period. was designed by Adam. It has the wheel ck. The seat is approximately semi-cular at back and sides.

SATINWOOD CHAIR. Late eighteenth century. Here we have the work of Sheraton. Whereas Chippendale had used carving almost exclusively, Sheraton preferred inlay and painting. The chief characteristic of his work was its lightness.

PAINTED CHAIR. Early nineteenth century. Sheraton's last designs were not so happy as his earlier efforts. Many disturbing influences were at work. This chair is of the Trafalgar Period, and is at the beginning of Victorian age.

FIRST AID IN THE HOME

EVERYONE should know how to deal with everyday accidents. Many a life has been lost through a cut being neglected. By first aid is meant help for accidents that cannot be foreseen. If a person faints constantly, there is something wrong, and a doctor will prescribe what is to be done for these attacks, but where a person has a fainting attack, maybe from hunger, fright or a hundred and one other causes, unprecedented and unexpected, one should have a simple remedy at hand and know how to use it.

SEND FOR THE DOCTOR

It is as well to remember that, except in very minor injuries, *the doctor should be sent for*, but much can be done, before the doctor arrives, to alleviate suffering and in some instances save life.

Simple Requisites to Keep in the House

The following are simple remedies which should be found in every household : —Some small sterilized dressings for injured fingers, also medium size for hands or feet, and large ones for other injured parts ; there should also be specially sterilized dressings—large, medium and small—for burns ; cotton-wool in $\frac{1}{2}$-oz. packets, a supply of lint and a sufficient number of suitable bandages. These should all be carefully wrapped and kept free from dust. A bottle of sal-volatile,

*Fig. 1.—*To Stop Bleeding.

An accidental cut on the palm of the hand can very quickly be stopped from bleeding by tightly grasping a tennis-ball, with sterilized dressings, while keeping the hand elevated.

with the dose and mode of administration indicated on label ; a bottle of smelling salts or hermetically sealed tubes filled with it and easy to carry in the pocket ; a bottle of 2 per cent. alcoholic solution of iodine or Friar's Balsam ; a stoppered bottle of crystals of permanganate of potash or Condy's Fluid or some other disinfectant. You will also require a medicine glass and a sharp pair of scissors. Place all these requisites in a cupboard *above* the level of children's reach, and keep it closed but not locked. Special things are required for different casualties, and these are mentioned under the headings of the following most common accidents.

WHAT TO DO IN CASE OF—

Fainting

Fainting being due to diminution of the blood supply to the brain from the loss of power of the heart, lay the patient flat on the back or raise the feet. Give fresh air and loosen clothing, apply smelling salts —hermetically-sealed tubes filled with liquid smelling salts can be carried in one's pocket—sprinkle cold water on the face, and, if able to swallow, give the patient water or a little diluted stimulant or sal-volatile. A fainting fit may be prevented by sitting a patient in a chair and bending his or her head down between the knees, taking care he does not fall.

Epileptic Fit

Do not restrain convulsive movements, but prevent patient from self-injury. Loosen tight clothing; prevent the tongue being bitten by placing hard substance between teeth.

Convulsions in Infants

Place the child in a warm bath for from ten to twenty minutes, or place its feet in warm water with mustard in it. Apply cold to the head.

Stings

For stings of insects, such as bees, wasps and gnats, apply solution of ammonia or bicarbonate of soda (a sodamint tablet which contains carbonate of ammonia is often at hand and can be easily crushed and applied). Warn the sufferer to refrain from scratching, as such action will drive the poison into the system. A solution of Epsom-salt 1 in 20 rubbed on the skin will keep off insects; eucalyptus oil will also act in a like manner.

Bites of Venomous and Rabid Animals

The wound should be immediately washed with clean water, warm in preference to encourage bleeding—cold and hot water stop bleeding. If a limb be the injured part, grasp it firmly above wound, tie tightly a handkerchief, necktie or piece of string round above the bite. If one has no cracks or sores about the lips or tongue, suck the wound and wash out your mouth with brandy or other spirit and water. A breast pump may be used for sucking the wound.

For a venomous animal's bite apply strong fluid solution of permanganate of potash or Condy's Fluid, or rub a crystal or two into the wound. In the case of bite from a supposedly mad dog, act as above, but two teaspoonfuls of carbolic acid with half a pint of water make a good lotion.

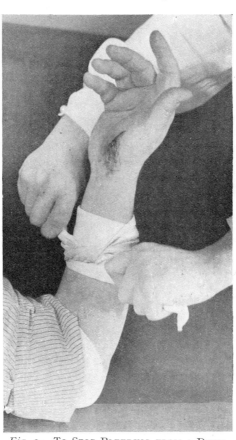

Cauterizing the wound on the surface with nitrate of silver is not sufficient to destroy poison: you must burn to the bottom. Give a stimulant if there be fainting, and artificial respiration if necessary.

Removal of Foreign Body from the Eye

Do not use any hard instrument; a camel's-hair brush or a piece of soft moistened linen should be adequate. In the lower lid pull down the eyelid. The upper lid may be everted by placing a match, bodkin or probe over it and then gently pulling the lid over. Do not rub the affected eye, but temporary relief until one is ready to act as above may be given by rubbing the non-affected eye, when possibly the tears in bad eye will

Fig. 2.—To Stop Bleeding from a Deep Cut.

A tightly-bound handkerchief or two above the cut will suffice to check it, especially if the arm is raised at the same time.

wash out the grit, etc. A mother can often remove a foreign body from her child's eye by inserting her tongue and licking around.

Wounds

It must be remembered that germs, microbes or bacteria which belong to the

If only a scratch or slight wound, omit the washing if not dirty, and apply iodine solution at once and allow to dry. Iodine sterilizes the wound and makes any dirt harmless.

Be careful not to keep on removing blood clots, as they prevent bleeding and keep out impurities.

There are several other drugs and chemical substances kept handy to kill and prevent the growth of germs (antiseptics)—Friars Balsam (undiluted), boric or boracic acid used as a powder or in a saturated solution in water; permanganate of potash, a few grains dissolved in water.

Inflammation

A cut may "fester," and the sore area will rapidly become red, hot and painful.

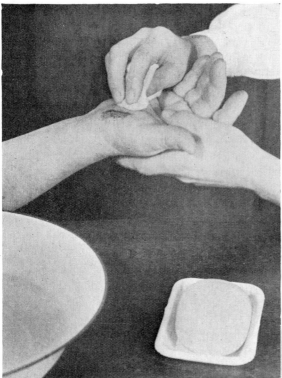

Fig. 3.—DON'T TREAT CUTS WITH CONTEMPT.

Remove the dirt present by washing with soap and water. Should the cut extend deeply and should there be dirt at the edge of the wound, it would be better to get medical assistance to remove this rather than allow it to get into the depths by injudicious prodding.

vegetable world exist everywhere and cannot be seen by the naked eye. Hands are never free from germs, so do not touch wounds, and when applying a "sterilized dressing" do not handle the part which is applied to the wound, and thoroughly wash your hands, if there be time, before dealing with the case. To prevent poisoning by a wound, keep it clean and aseptic (or germ-free). If a wound is dirty, it must be washed immediately; whisky or methylated spirits with an equal bulk of water may be used.

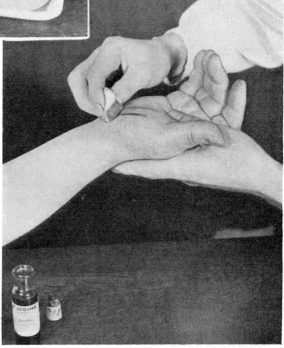

Fig. 4.—DEALING WITH A CUT.

Should an antiseptic be at hand, such as iodine, apply it to the cut and cover the part over.

The ideal treatment for the condition is to *rest* the part. If it is the arm, put it into a sling; if the leg, the patient is put to bed. But naturally such extreme measures will not often be needed.

The wounded area should be fomented, and if scabs tend to form these should be carefully removed after washing in hot water so that discharges do not collect underneath them. The fomentations should be used every four hours. The best way to prepare and use the fomentation is shown in Figs. 7 to 12.

Bleeding (Hæmorrhage)

In all cases keep patient quiet. To temporarily arrest external bleeding, apply pressure with the finger or thumb over a piece of sterilized dressing or clean linen, or tightly apply over them a bandage. If the blood be bright red (arterial), apply pressure between the heart and the wound; if the blood be dark (venous), apply on the side away from the heart. Cold water or ice application will assist. Hot water, hotter than the hand can comfortably bear, is more effectual than cold water. Warm water is useless, as it encourages the bleeding.

Bleeding from the Nose

Should not be stopped too soon; it is sometimes salutary, especially in aged people, relieving congestion of the brain. Seat the patient with his head thrown back, not leaning over a basin. Hold the hands as high as possible above and behind the head and keep them there. Open the windows. If severe, apply cold to the back of the neck and between shoulder blades; use a cold wet sponge, towel, or a lump of ice. Do not blow the nose; pinch the front of the organ in case the bleeding

Fig. 5.—NEVER RUB THE EYES TO REMOVE GRIT.

If you do not know how to lift the lids clear for that purpose, close the eyes and let the tears wash away the dirt. A sufficient flow of tears may be ensured, as is well known, by getting close to a sliced onion!

comes from the forepart. Sniffing up vinegar and water or lemon-juice and water may be tried.

Burns, Scalds and Shock

To extinguish burning clothing, lay the person down and roll him in a coat, shawl, rug, blanket, thick curtain or any such handy article. Give stimulants in small quantities if there be shock, and be sure the patient is conscious enough to swallow. Shock in children can be counteracted by hot baths.

Clothing must be removed with the greatest care from the injured parts, so that no blisters are broken. If clothing adheres, it should be removed after soaking with warm water in which is a sprinkle of boracic acid, or leave the adherent clothing and immerse, if possible, the damaged part in a bath, or bathe with warm water to which some bicarbonate of soda has been added. This will help to remove any charred clothing.

The object to be aimed at is to protect the injured surfaces from the air by using a dressing of vaseline (aseptic) containing some boracic acid; carbolic oil 1 in 10 can be used, also eucalyptus oil; place over the dressing several layers of cotton-wool. Do not prick a blister; never apply any ointment or oil which has not been rendered sterile or does not contain a disinfectant.

Children have been known to suck water from the spout of a boiling kettle of water: apply fomentations to the neck and downwards, give ice to suck and keep patient sitting up.

Other Burns

For burns due to contact with acids or alkalis, pour *plenty* of water over the part

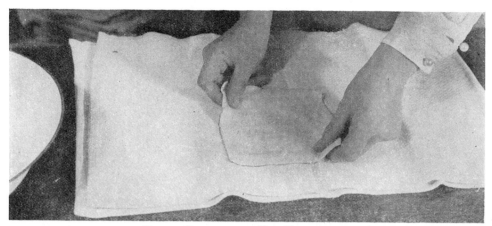

Fig. 7.—PREPARING A HOT FOMENTATION.
Take a piece of boracic lint of a size sufficient to cover the inflamed area
and lay it on a face towel.

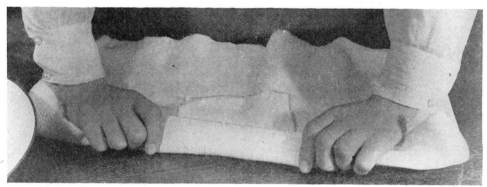

Fig. 8.—PREPARING A HOT FOMENTATION.
Then roll up the lint in the towel.

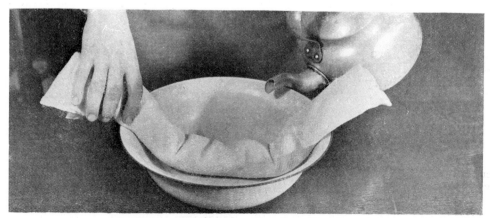

Fig. 9.—PREPARING A HOT FOMENTATION.
Immerse the part where the lint is in boiling water.

Fig. 10.—PREPARING A HOT FOMENTATION.
Wring the towel and lint as dry as you can.

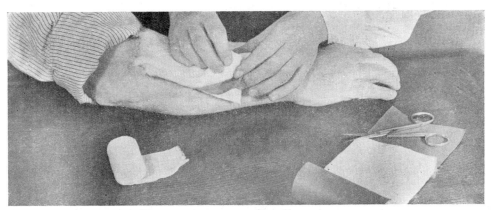

Fig. 11.—APPLYING A HOT FOMENTATION.
Gently place the heated lint on the affected part, cover the lint with a piece of oil-silk, and over
that place a thick piece of cotton-wool.

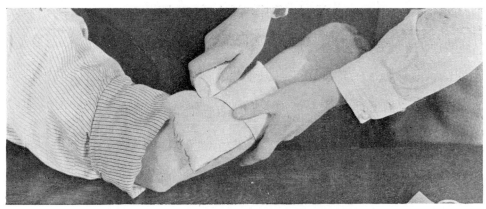

Fig. 12.—BANDAGING ON A HOT FOMENTATION.

to get rid of any surplus. Then, for acids, wash to neutralise with a solution of washing soda. For alkalis, use vinegar water. Treat as ordinary burns.

Fractures

are recognised by the pain generally referred to by the patient at the point at which the bone is broken. There are swelling, loss of power, alteration in shape, and unnatural mobility. There is also crepitus, i.e., a grating sensation when the broken ends of the bone are rubbed against each other. If there be any doubt about a fracture, treat the case as being one. Use the greatest gentleness to prevent further injury, so as not to cause the ends to pierce the skin, thereby converting a simple into a compound fracture. Do not drag off clothing.

Leg

In the case of a leg, unfasten braces, split the outside seam of the trousers and draw the cut garment to the inside of the injured limb, and then the trousers can be pulled off ; to remove the boot, slit up the back seam and cut off the sock.

Upper Limbs

In fracture of the upper limbs, rip up the coat seams and shirt. If unnecessary, do not attempt to move a patient before the arrival of a doctor. In no case should there be removal until splints have been applied. A fractured upper extremity may be supported in a sling and tied to the side. The lower limbs should be tied together at the knees and ankles, the sound leg acting as splint. Bags filled with sand and placed on each side are useful to prevent movement.

Compound Fracture

In a compound fracture it will be necessary to remove the clothing, more especially if there be hæmorrhage. Apply pressure to the artery above the injury ; cover up the wound with a clean pad of sterilized dressing or linen which has been boiled for five minutes, and then soaked in a disinfectant—solution of boracic. For cleansing use well-boiled water allowed to cool, to which has been added two tablespoonfuls of Condy's fluid or common salt, a dessertspoonful in a tumbler of water.

Fig. 6.—TREATING BURNS FROM HOT FAT.

If skin be unbroken the burn should be at once smothered with flour. This is always handy in the kitchen, and is as suitable a dressing as anything if nothing else be handy.

Injury to Ribs

Apply bandages firmly round the chest.

Fractured Collar Bone

is generally recognised by the deformity in the line of the bone. Place a wedge-shaped pad in the armpit, base upwards. The arm close to the side, forearm across the chest, the hand pointing to the opposite shoulder ; place forearm in a sling and fix arm to the side of the body. Knots should always be made to tie on sound side.

Dislocation

This always happens at a joint but, of

course, it may be combined with a fracture. In a dislocation there is unnatural stiffness of the joint, which distinguishes it from a fracture. No attempt at reduction should be made, but a surgeon sent for immediately.

Electric Shock

If there be contact with cable or wire, switch off current if possible and free the patient, but whilst sufferer is in contact he must not be touched by the naked hands of the rescuer, unless the latter be insulated upon an india-rubber mat or pile of *dry* clothes. Push the sufferer away with a piece of dry wood, or catch hold of him by covering hand with an empty india-rubber tobacco pouch. India-rubber gloves are of course better, but not always handy. Dry clothing or a mackintosh coat can be thrown around patient, but do not touch his clothing which may be damp. If necessary, perform artificial respiration, and do not cease until patient comes under medical attention. Treat burns in usual manner.

Gas Poisoning and Fumes from Exhausts

Remove to fresh air, loosen tight clothing and use artificial respiration. Continue for four or five hours before hope is lost. That there are no signs of life must not act as a deterrent.

Choking

Force open the mouth and endeavour to hook out with the forefinger the obstructing body. Hold up children by their legs and thump between the shoulder blades. This can also be tried with adults.

Frost Bite

Do not apply heat, but rub the part with snow or cold water so as to thaw gradually. Do not resort to the fire or go into a warm room.

Poisons

Individually, these are not being dealt with in this article, but emetics must not be given in corrosive poisons or those which eat away tissues such as acids or alkalis. If the poison be a corrosive acid give lime water or chalk and water, linseed or olive oil. If an alkali, give weak vinegar and water or lime juice. A handy emetic is a tablespoonful of mustard in a tumbler of warm water, also salt—two tablespoonfuls in a tumbler of warm water—but salt must not be given if sulphate of zinc has been used as an emetic.

Sunstroke

Remove to a cool place, loosen all tight clothing, provide plenty of fresh air, douche head, neck, chest and spine or whole of the body with cold water. Give cold water to drink, but no stimulant.

Exposure to Infection

This refers to scarlet fever, diphtheria, measles, etc. Gargle the throat as soon as possible with a solution of permanganate of potash—a few grains to a tumbler of tepid water, enough to give it a pink colour—also douche the inside of the nose by placing some of the water in the palm of the hand, drawing it through the nostrils and expelling through the mouth. Gargling in such a manner night and morning, or as frequently as possible, is a good preventive during an influenza epidemic, as the poison of the disease is easily destroyed. If feeling ill during an epidemic go to bed, keep warm and send for a medical man.

Sprains.

A sprain has been designated as a "missed dislocation," there being an absence of special signs of dislocation or fracture. Literally, sprains are twisting or wrenching of a joint with more or less injury to the adjacent muscles and tendons. There is also straining or tearing of the capsule of a joint or of the ligaments. Pain is severe and increased by movement, there is inability to bear weight on the injured limb, loss of power, swelling round the joint often followed by black and blue discoloration (bruising), owing to effusion of blood into and around the joint.

The first essential is absolute rest for the injured part. In case of the lower limb, the patient must not attempt to walk and the limb must be kept elevated ;

Fig. 13.—PREVENTION IS BETTER THAN CURE.
It's better to avoid the risk of electric shock than to court it at any time by switching on the light while the hand is wet. Such an action may cause a short-circuit on the switch, which would give rise to a shock then or subsequently. With a short-circuit of this nature, and a person holding a wet object, such as a wash basin, with the other hand, there is serious risk. To do this while in a bath has caused death. Never touch electrical gear while wet!

whilst an upper extremity should be placed in a sling. Cloths wrung out in cold water and kept wet should be applied to the injured part, or an ice bag or evaporating lotions can be used. The application of cold prevents inflammation and arrests bleeding ; sometimes very hot water—as hot as can be borne—or the application of bran poultices relieves the pain.

Sprained Ankle

" Going over of the ankle " is a common expression for an ordinary sprain of that joint. If such an accident occurs when one is far from help or assistance of any kind, the best way to prevent swelling is to lace the boot up tightly. If a lace-up boot is not worn, do not remove the shoe or stocking, but bind the foot and ankle tightly round with a bandage (if you have one with you) otherwise use a strap, handkerchief or scarf, etc. After reaching shelter or destination, do not drag off the boot and stocking, but if necessary cut both off carefully.

Strains

Strains are caused by overstretching of tendons or muscles, through pulling or lifting heavy weights or other severe exertion. The pain is sharp or acute, making movement impossible or difficult and painful. The first step is to place the patient as comfortably as possible, and relief can often be afforded by the application of hot fomentations or hot-water bottles.

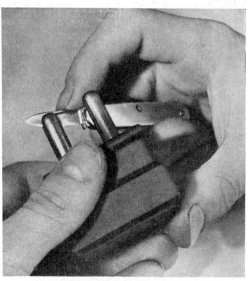

Fig. 14.—To PREVENT ACCIDENTS TO
INQUISITIVE CHILDREN.
A spare plug without any flex can be inserted in the switch as a dummy. To make it a tight fit, that only a grown-up can remove, open the slits in the pins slightly.

MAKING A PANELLED LAMP SHADE
EXPLAINING HOW TO USE THE HOME CONSTRUCTION CHART

Fig. 1.—THE LAMP SHADE IN USE.

This and other attractive shades like it can easily be made and decorated by the reader, even if he or she possesses no artistic ability, by following the instructions contained in this article and on the Home Construction Chart.

I WONDER how many times many of us have gazed in windows and at lamp-shade departments in the large stores, and longed for at least one of the beautifully shaped vellum shades displayed there. More often than not, we can find one to suit every room in the house, but oh ! The price !

Now, no one with normally nimble fingers need ever be without decorative shades in their homes, as I hope the following article and the Home Construction Chart amply shows.

Obtain a Suitable Wire Frame

Before going to the maker of the wire frames which, of course, is the first thing you will need, be sure you know the size of the shade you require. The size is measured across the bottom, and in a hanging or pendant shade, or one for a standard lamp, usually range from 12 inches to 18 inches across ; larger ones can be obtained if required. A reading-lamp size is about 8 or 10 inches. A mistake that is often made, is that it is easier to make one of the round shades, that is, one of the shapes with just a ring top and bottom, than to make one of the more elaborate panelled shapes, but such is not the case, and we all know there is no comparison in the effectiveness of the latter.

Should the wire maker not have the shape you require in stock he will always make one to any size and design you may wish. The six-panelled frame described here can be obtained from Heinson Bros., 45–50 Whitfield St., London, W. 1. These wires are very reasonable in price.

Bind the Wire Frame

Having obtained the wire shape, the next thing to do is to bind it. This is necessary, for as you will see later, the vellum is stitched to this binding. Mercerised lawn makes a very good binding, as it frays less easily than silk and is firmer for the vellum. Cut the lawn in strips, on the cross, about $1\frac{1}{4}$ inch to $1\frac{1}{2}$ inch wide, and if you give these strips a good hard pull each end, the sides will usually turn in naturally, so the cut edges will be made neat without the bother of ironing.

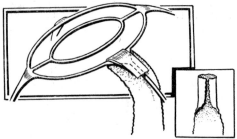
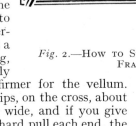

Fig. 2.—How to Start Binding the Frame.

How to Bind the Frame Neatly

A great thing to remember is that the inside of the shade must be kept neat, as it can always be seen by anyone looking up, and any little untidiness or un-professional look is sure to be spotted by some friend, especially if they know you have made the shade yourself! This being so, when you start binding the bars bring the folded end of the strip of lawn on to the outside of the bar, as you see in Fig. 2, and stitch very firmly at the top and then proceed to cover the bar, making each twist just touch and not cover the one going before (see Fig. 3). It is essential not to cover the bars thickly, as, when the shade has the light behind it, they will look clumsy. Cut the strips of lawn quite on the cross, as this allows you to pull the material well down the bar. When you have bound the bar in this way, to finish off, bring the end of the strip on to the outside of the wire, as you did at the top, and again stitch it very firmly before cutting off any material you may have left over.

Now the Base of the Frame

Do all the bars in this

Fig. 3.—Binding the Frame.
Neaten the lawn strip binding as shown.

way, and then start binding the base of the shade. For this, have a long strip of lawn (still on the cross), if possible, long enough to go right round the shade. But if this cannot be done, be sure and join the material at the end of the bars, as it will then not slip. Go on binding as before, taking care that the bar ends are made quite neat ; one usually has to wrap this part twice or three times tightly so as to get the wire covered properly. After this, bind the top ring, in fact the only part left unbound is the small ring, which fits on the electric holder and the tiny bars branching from it which hold the rest of the shade. It looks better, if white material is used for the binding, to tint it the colour of the vellum with either coloured ink or water-colours.

Cutting Vellum to Shape

Now for the actual covering of the shade. It is surprising how much can be done with a shilling sheet of vellum, if cut with care. It will cover a 12-inch six-panelled shade, as in Fig. 1.

First cut a piece off the sheet of vellum rather larger than one of the panels. Place this piece of vellum over the wire and pencil down one side of it the shape of the wire bar which can be seen through the vellum, cut along the pencilled line with sharp scissors, then put this edge to the centre of the bar as in Fig. 4, and stitch. The reason for putting the vellum just to the centre of the bar is so that the edge of the panels shall not, as far as possible, overlap each other in the sewing on. If they did, it would look so lumpy when covered by the braid or gimp.

Stitching on the Vellum Panels

The panels are sewn on

with buttonhole- or blanket-stitch, but, unlike the usual method of working this stitch when you hold the edge of the work towards you, in this case hold the edge away from you and do the finishing off of the stitch on the inside instead of on the outside edge. Fig. 4 will show the way to hold the shade and the stitching.

It is advisable to work the blanket-stitch the opposite way to that usually done. It preserves the edge of the paper, which is liable to split if pulled too hard at the edge. This is why it is also better to make the stitches a good way apart, from $\frac{1}{2}$ inch to $\frac{3}{4}$ inch, so that should one stitch tear the paper it is easy to put in another.

Do as little sewing as possible on the actual paper itself, so long as you make it firm and not likely to break away from the bars.

The one side of the panel fixed securely, pencil down the other side of the vellum on the next bar, cut and sew in the same way. With two sides once on, the most important part of the panelling is over. Now cut the vellum to the shape of the top and the bottom of the wire frame,

Fig. 4.—How to Stitch the Vellum to the Frame.

and buttonhole-stitch in the usual way, that is, bringing the buttonholing to the edge of the paper. Put all the other panels on in the same way.

Cut Each Panel Separately

You will find it safer to cut each panel separately and *not* to make a pattern of the first one, then cut the others from it, because should the wires differ a fraction of an inch, or you happen to move slightly the bar in the binding or sewing on the vellum, all your other cut-out panels will be wasted. For the sewing use strong white cotton, not thread.

Finishing with Braid or Gimp

There only remains now the putting on of the braid or gimp, to cover your stitches on the bars and to add to the general decoration. Either silk or metal gimp can be used, and can be bought very cheaply at most drapers or stores. Again, in this finishing off, you want to do as little sewing as possible, so cut off pieces of gimp the length of the bars and make a crease down the centre of the pieces. Turn in the raw edge at the top to make it neat and stitch firmly on to the top of the bar. Pull hard so that the crease in the centre of the gimp fits exactly over the curve of the bar, and again stitch it well at the bottom after turning under the end. The sewing at the top and bottom of the bar should be quite enough to hold the gimp firm, unless it is a very big shade, when it may need just a stitch in the middle of the curve. When all the bars are covered there are just the top and bottom wires to do. Crease the gimp in the same way, but not quite in the centre, to make one side a little wider than the other. Keep this wider side on the vellum and let the narrower side go just round the wire. Start the sewing at a bar, and oversew the narrow edge on to the wire, making the gimp fit tightly by mitreing it at each of the bars.

For stitching on the gimp use a yellow or natural-coloured cotton, so that stitches will not show on the metal or silk. Should still more decoration be needed, coloured beads and tassels can be added to the points according to individual taste.

Decorating the Shade

Now, for anyone who likes painting and colour, comes the most exciting part of shade making, and that is the decoration of the shade itself.

This can be done in many ways. It can be stencilled; always a good formal form of decoration especially when applied to a large article. It can be shaded in graduated tints, with lamp-shade colours. Again, the shade can be painted in artist's oil-colours, only, if working with these, care must be taken to use only the transparent colours, as otherwise the colours look muddy when the light is behind them. Best of all, I think, are the shades painted with Winsor & Newton's coloured waterproof inks. These can be obtained in numerous delightful colours which are absolutely transparent.

Putting on the Design

But before we get to the colouring, we must put the design on to the lamp shade. Choose a design in keeping with the other decorations in the room, both in style and colour. If one has the gift of being able to draw one's own designs, there are many to choose from in the shops, and sometimes a needlework design can be adapted to suit the panels of the shade. Trace the design on to tracing paper thereby keeping the original from getting torn, place a piece of coloured carbon paper—this can be bought in red, blue, etc.— face down on the vellum, and over that the traced design, and then draw the design with a rather sharp point, such as a well-sharpened pencil or end of a knitting needle, etc., taking care not to press hard enough to tear the paper. Lift the paper, now and again, to see that the design has come off clearly, but not thickly.

How to Paint the Shade

The design on, now start the painting. You may find it a little awkward at first holding the shade whilst painting, but if you put your arm up the inside of the shade and hold through the ring at the top, the shade will be quite firm

and, after a little while, you will get used to it. It is always safer to make a shade up first before painting, as it is so easy to pull the panel slightly askew when stitching them on the wires, and, if the design is already on, it puts the whole decoration wrong. A great thing to remember in painting lamp shades is that the colours must look well in both the day and artificial light, so while you are painting, keep holding the shade up to the light and see which colours are lost with the light behind them. Should the painting look just right by daylight, but weak in electric light, paint the predominating colours on the inside of the shade as well as on the front. In this way the shade does not look crude and highly coloured in daytime, but gets the extra colour shown through when lit up. Another thing which adds to the clearness of your design is always to outline your painting with either black or brown ink. Should you want merely to tint the vellum on your shade, first of all paint it over with lamp-shade medium. When this is dry, paint on your lamp-shade colour with a wash-brush all over the shade, leave it for a few moments and then rub well in with a pad of cotton-wool or soft rag, until no gummy substance is left. Hold the shade up to the light, and if the yellowness of the vellum alters the tone of the colour, tint the whole of the inside of the shade as well. This tinting in pale colours makes a charming background for silhouettes or a black design.

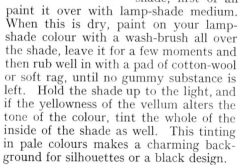

Fig. 5.—Used as a Hanging Shade.

CROSS-STITCH EMBROIDERY

Fig. 1.—A Simple Piece of Work in Cross-Stitch.

Instructions for making this table runner are given in the text. A chart of the pattern is given in Fig. 1A.

OF all the forms of embroidery, there is none more popular or fascinating than cross-stitch. Owing to its simplicity it provides one of the most effective methods of decorative stitchery.

In bygone days, it formed part of the training of every well educated girl, and

museums are evidence of the interest and skill devoted to this craft. Due mainly to the many beautiful threads that are now manufactured, there is a wide field for choice in pattern and colour.

Fabrics to Decorate with Cross-Stitch

Almost any kind of fabric may be

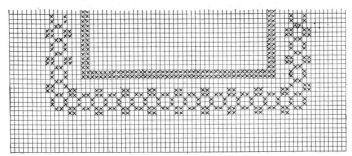

Fig. 1A.—Chart for the Table Runner shown in Fig. 1.

Crosses indicate the stitches. Methods of working cross-stitches are shown on the next page.

the exquisitely executed samplers that are to be seen in many homes and

embroidered with cross-stitch. For the beginner, there are specially-prepared

CROSS-STITCH EMBROIDERY

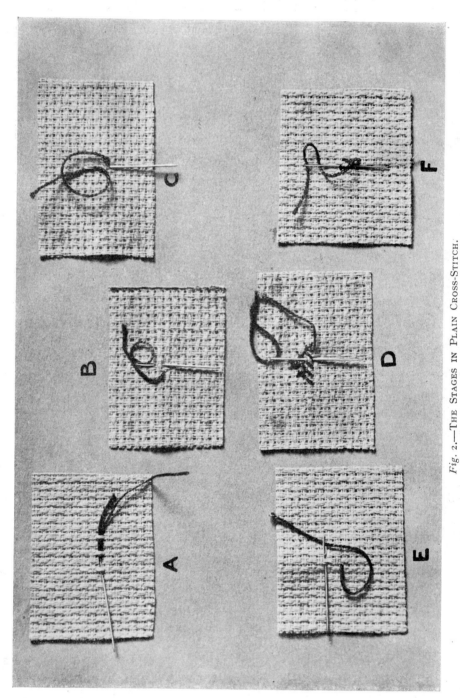

Fig. 2.—THE STAGES IN PLAIN CROSS-STITCH.

A, the beginning of the stitch at the back of the material. B, the first stroke. C, completing the plain cross-stitch. D, another method, forming a line of cross-stitches. E, making a long cross-stitch, first stage. F, completing long stitch.

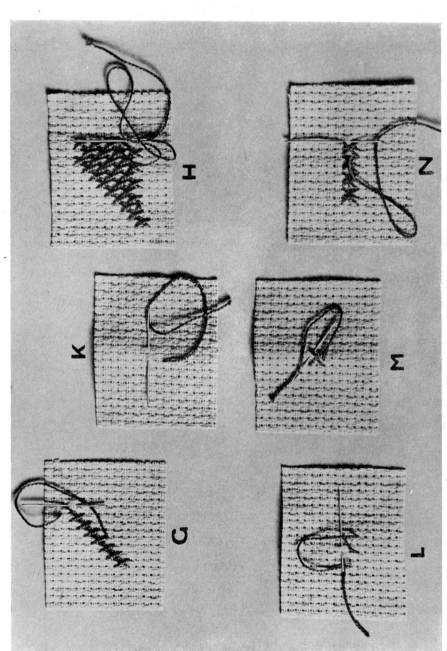

Fig. 3.—Some More Details of Cross-Stitch, Showing a Method of Filling Up and the Stages in the Double Stitch. G, completed series of long cross-stitches, and also method of doing them. H, the use of these stitches in filling up spaces. K, the first stage of working the double cross-stitch. L, second stage. M, third stage, and N, the completion of the double cross-stitch, and a series of them.

design can be quite easily applied with a transfer.

Methods of Applying Pattern

As cross-stitch depends for its effect on the use of squares, it is necessary that the arrangement of the pattern should allow of diagonal stitches, which should be crossed always in the same direction. As a rule, transfers on well defined weaves, such as canvas, are not needed. On cloth or closely woven materials, the pattern may be worked on penelope canvas tacked in position, and the threads of the canvas withdrawn when the work is finished, leaving the cross-stitch on the material.

Fig. 4.—A BIB FOR BABY IS EASILY DECORATED IN CROSS-STITCH.

See the chart for working details on the next page (Fig. 6).

canvases showing distinct and easily counted threads. Linen and huckaback are other suitable materials. In the case of closely woven fabrics, such as dress materials and fine linen, in which it is difficult or impossible to count the threads the pattern for the

Fig. 5.—A CORNER OF AN AFTERNOON TEA CLOTH.

Worked with " Star Sylko " in two colours.

Threads and Needle to Use

There are many kinds of threads that are suitable, crewel, tapestry and other embroidery wools, mercerised cotton in a large variety of colours, linen threads in several different makes, and there is a large choice in embroidery silks, both real and artificial. The needle used is the ordinary crewel needle with a blunt point. Care should be taken that the thread washes well and is a fast colour. For this reason cheap threads should be avoided.

Working-Out the Pattern—How to Begin

The method employed in working-out the pattern is shown at Fig. 2. The beginning of the stitch, starting it at the back of the material, is shown at A. This is necessary as knots must be avoided.

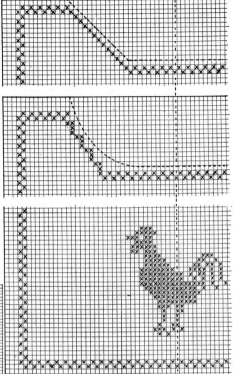

Fig. 6. — CHART FOR THE CROSS-STITCH BIB, SHOWN IN FIG. 4.

The needle is brought out at the lower corner of the square and carried across to the opposite corner, as at B. The stitch is completed by bringing the needle to the top left - hand c o r n e r, a n d when brought out again, as shown at C, the needle is ready for the first stitch of the next square.

Fig. 7.—CHART FOR THE CORNER DESIGN FOR A TEA CLOTH, SHOWN IN FIG. 5.

Two styles of marking indicate the two colours used.

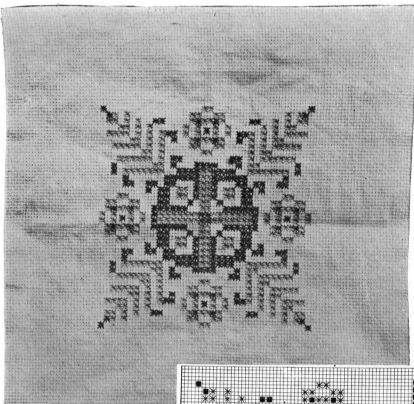

Fig 8.—A Cushion Square Worked in Orange and Black "Star Sylko."

to show the sides. The edges are turned in and finished underneath by slip-stitching.

Another example of simple work is shown in Fig. 4, and provides an opportunity for practice in filling up long rows. The same kind of canvas is used, but the edges are

An Embroidered Table Runner

The example is worked in pale and darker saxe-blue "Star Sylko," Nos. 768 and 771, Size 5, on coarse cross-stitch canvas and is shown in Fig. 1. It is suitable either for a table runner or duchesse set, and is a simple piece of work for a beginner. The canvas should be cut off to a width of 12 inches for a duchesse set, or 18 inches for a table runner, from a 42-inch width. The design can be followed from the chart at Fig. 1A, which shows one complete end and sufficient

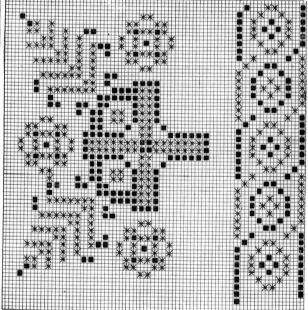

Fig. 9.—Chart for Working out the Cushion Pattern shown in Fig. 8.

The border pattern shown here is suitable for use with the centre design. Both designs are in double cross-stitch.

Fig. 10.—ANOTHER TABLE RUNNER EMBROIDERED IN CROSS-STITCH.
The filling shown at H in Fig. 3 is used for this design.

Fig. 11.—AN ELABORATE PIECE OF CROSS-STITCH SHOWING THE BACKGROUND FILLED IN.

turned in $\frac{1}{2}$ inch first and lightly tacked. The design is shown on the chart in Fig. 6, and gives one half with the bird decoration and the stitching for the top. An alternative design for a curved border is also shown on the chart.

An Afternoon Tea Cloth

One of the advantages of cross-stitch is the adaptability of the pattern unit. It can be used as a separate corner design or carried on as a border, and the stitch may cover four squares instead of one. An example of what is possible in direction is shown in the bold design in Fig. 5, and represents the corner of an afternoon tea cloth stitched in brown and gold. The border is plainly hemmed, using the slip-stitch, but to give variety, the threads may be drawn.

In the design chart in Fig. 7, the squares to be filled in with gold are indicated by crossed lines, and those done with brown, by black squares. The same pattern is equally effective when worked in single squares in one colour only. The example in Fig. 5 was worked in " Star Sylko," Nos. 805 and 702, Size 5.

Filling in Large Spaces

It is not always necessary, or advisable, to use the ordinary cross-stitch. In many designs it is necessary to fill up comparatively large spaces, either in the design as shown in Fig. 10, or as a means of dealing with the background as indicated in Fig. 11. In both cases the actual lines of the pattern are done in ordinary cross-stitch, but the filling is done with the long-stitch.

The Long-Stitch

The method of working the long-stitch is shown in Fig. 2. Beginning as at A with the thread passed through the material, the needle misses one square and is carried through the mesh above,

as shown at E. The stitch is completed as indicated at F, and each successive stitch done in the same way. A completed length of long-stitches is shown at G in Fig. 3. The illustration at H gives an indication of the use of the stitch in filling up : it will be seen that the beginning of each new stitch is on the next square above, and not the second square, as in ordinary cross-stitch. In filling up definite spaces with the long-stitch it will, of course, be necessary to use the ordinary cross-stitch in every other row, to keep the bottom row level, but the easier way is to work across the material, as shown, whenever it is possible. This method can be worked equally well on the slant or the upright.

Double Cross-Stitch

A pleasing variation is the double cross-stitch, which is the ordinary diagonal stitch with a straight cross worked over it. It is quite a good method of working out a bold pattern, using, of course, four squares. The effect of the stitch is shown in the cushion square in Fig. 8, which is worked on coarse canvas in orange and black " Star Sylko," No. 867.

The planning of the pattern is shown in the draft in Fig. 9, which gives half the design as well as a suitable border which can be used with it if desired. The portion stitched with orange is indicated by cross lines, the solid squares signify the black stitches. The method of working the double stitch is shown in stages in Fig. 3. The first stage at K shows the needle in the ordinary position, which is completed by the stitch at L, but the needle is brought out in the next square, so that it can be carried down to the same point below, as shown at M, which shows the position of the needle for the final stitch. The full effect of the stitch is shown at N.

MODERN LIGHTING IN THE HOME

USING GAS OR ELECTRIC LIGHT

*Fig. 1.—*BESIDE THE FIRESIDE ARMCHAIR.
An electric standard placed in a position to give the greatest amount of fireside
comfort.   (Best & Lloyd, Ltd.)

THE two most generally adopted forms of artificial lighting are electricity and gas. Modern improved methods of oil lighting and artistically shaped and coloured candles also have their uses ; but either gas or electricity is the main illuminant with the great majority of people.

Gas or Electric Light ?

Choosing between the two is by no means easy. In many houses other than new ones it will be found that gas lighting is already installed. In any event gas is still quite an economical form of lighting in most districts, although electricity can run it very close, especially if low-powered lamps are used at as many points as possible.

Gas Lighting—Enormous Improvements

It is not always realised that gas lighting has made enormous progress in the last few years. The artistic quality of the fittings has been greatly improved and all tendency towards glare, which is the concentration of too much light in one spot, has been eliminated.

Gas Fittings now Similar in Appearance to Electric

These improvements have been effected by several means. The newest burners are fitted with superheaters which give out considerably increased light ; and a new heat-resisting glass known as " Vitreosil " is used for bowls and globes. This heat-proof glass has made it possible

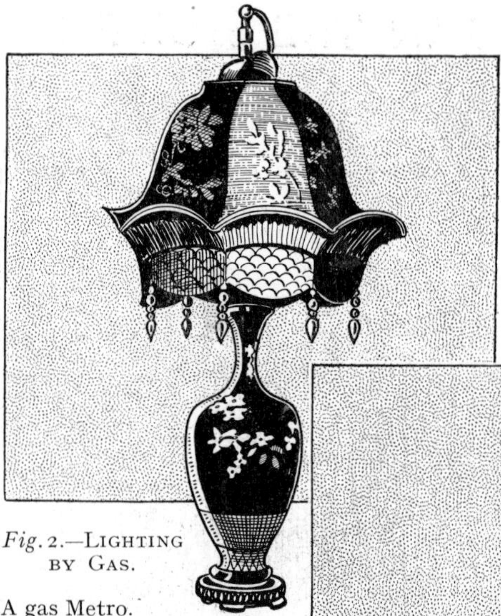

Fig. 2.—LIGHTING
BY GAS.

A gas Metro.
" Cloisonne " table lamp·

on each evening at each separate fitting
and lit laboriously with match or taper.
It can be turned on and off from a switch
conveniently situated near the door.
Switches for gas lighting, which are found
very reliable in practice, are operated by
direct mechanical action and with the
aid of a by-pass.

With good modern fittings gas has
pleasant colour and softness, and by
warming the atmo-
sphere near the ceiling
and causing the air to
circulate, gas also has
a healthy effect in help-
ing to ventilate the
room. Gas is, of
course, easy and inex-
pensive to install, and
one also has to bear
in mind the low cost
of gas mantles when
renewal becomes
necessary. Mantles,
too, are far less fragile
than they used to be.

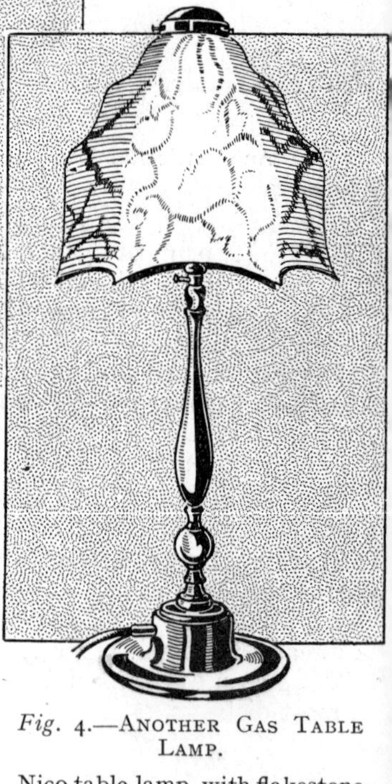

for gas lighting to be employed by the indirect
or reflected method
which was first adopted
for use with high-
powered electric lamps.
This glass makes it
possible to obtain the
maximum of lighting
efficiency without dan-
ger of the bowl being
broken by the heat
thrown off by the
burner. Consequently
it is possible to have
pendants and wall brac-
kets all designed for
indirect illumination
and very similar in
appearance to electric
fittings. Indeed, gas
can now be used with
practical and artistic
satisfaction for any
style and type of fitting.
There are gas floor and

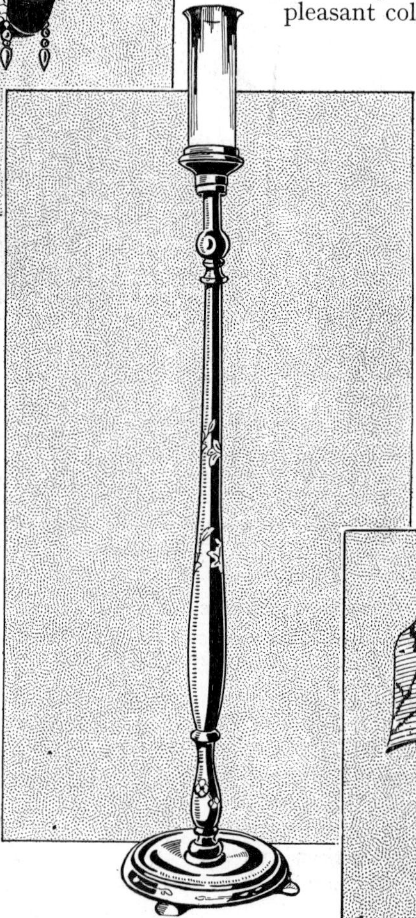

Fig. 3.—A GAS FLOOR
STANDARD LAMP.

These pictures show that
artistic lighting fittings are not
the monopoly of electric lighting.

table standards, and some charming gas candle
brackets with parchment or vellum shades harmonising admirably with period decoration and furnishing.

Switching on the Gas

Nor is it any longer necessary for gas to be turned

Fig. 4.—ANOTHER GAS TABLE
LAMP.

Nico table lamp, with flakestone
gold or pink veined glass shade.

The use of gas for lighting eliminates the necessity for dual supplies in the home (i.e., of both electric cable and wiring, and of gas mains and services), for whatever form of lighting be adopted, it is likely that gas will be used at any rate for part of the cooking.

As for the superheated burners just referred to, in these fittings the gas and air mixture is heated in a small chamber above the mantle on its way to the burner nozzle, and this results in an increase in the light given out.

Fitting the House with Electric Supply

One great advantage of electricity is its safety, especially in homes where there are children ; and it is the designers of electric fittings and shades, more than

Fig. 5.—A Gas Lighting Wall-Fitting in Shaded Glass.

anyone else, who have done so much to popularise really beautiful and artistic effects in lighting. In districts where there is an electricity supply corporation, and very few places are without one nowadays, there is rarely any difficulty in having an existing house wired for electric light. The work may cost from £10 or £12 upwards, according to the size, character and situation of the house, and the wiring can be very cleverly concealed. A good method is for the wiring to be run along the skirting boards of the walls and round the architraves of doors. It can then be painted to match the woodwork.

In an Existing House

Where it is desired to install wall lights in an existing house, a good way of treating the wiring is to run it up perpendicularly from the skirting and box it in with wood, thereby giving to the wall bracket the appearance of a mock floor standard.

How to Get the Best Lighting

More than half the secret of good lighting, whether gas or electricity be used, is in having lights at a number of different

Fig. 6.—A Gas Lighting Pendant.
An attractive modern fitting with glass panels in a framework of " stainless " metal.

Fig. 7.—Electric Lighting in the Lounge.

This lounge is lit by two wall lights, a pendant in polished aluminium and brass, a table lamp of modern design and a floor standard. The fire is a "Rippleray" electric. (Best & Lloyd, Ltd.)

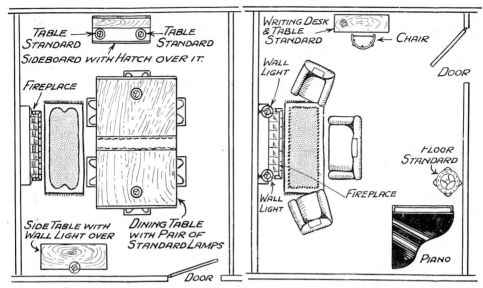

Fig. 8.—DINING-ROOM.   *Fig.* 8A.—SITTING-ROOM.

Figs. 8 and 8A.—POSITIONS FOR OCCASIONAL LAMPS, IN ADDITION TO THE
PRINCIPAL CEILING PENDANT.

points in the room. Generally, the main lighting should be from a pendant in the centre of the ceiling, and additional illumination should be provided by means of floor and table standards and wall brackets placed here and there. This is not such an extravagance as it may sound.

Without Extravagance

In the case of electricity, a real economy may be effected if lamps of lower power are used for the accessory positions.

Fig. 9.—" SWITCHING "
ON THE GAS.

With this switch, it is no longer necessary to go to the trouble of " lighting the gas."

There will often be occasions, such as when listening-in to wireless, or when smoking and talking, when one or two of the latter provide all the illumination needed. Fifteen-watt lamps can be used for these secondary positions ; and if

the house is a small one 15-watt lamps are also suitable for the front door, hall corridor, first floor landing, bathroom, w.c., and children's and servants' bedrooms. For the central position in dining-room, sitting-room and principal bedroom a 30-watt lamp should be sufficient if the room is not larger than 12 feet by 12 feet. For interiors larger than this a 40-watt or 60-watt lamp would be necessary.

Electric Light—In the Dining-Room

Let us consider the various rooms of the house one by one. Beginning with the dining-room, the central ceiling pendant should have a deep shade and should either be adjustable or be hung fairly low — just a

Fig. 9A.—A FLUSH
FITTING GAS SWITCH.

6—2

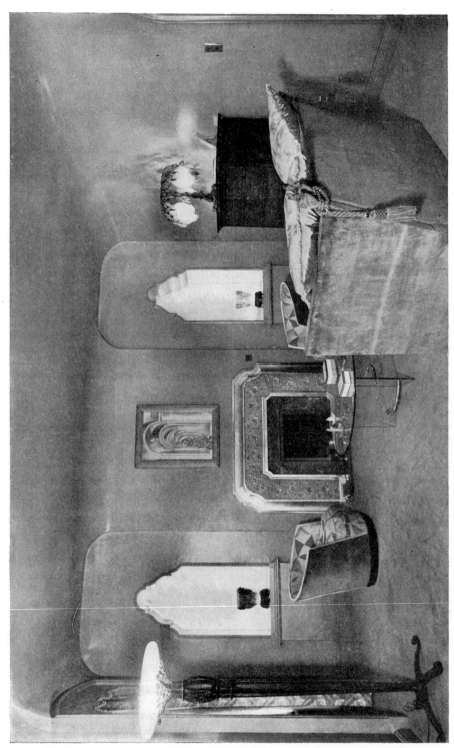

Fig. 10.—A WELL-LIT MODERN LOUNGE.
With electric floor and table standards and illuminated niches.

few inches above the heads of the diners. A pearl-finished electric lamp should be used, say 30 watts. This should have the effect of flooding the dining-table with clear light while leaving the rest of the room somewhat in shadow. The custom of including a pair of wall brackets on the dining-room chimneybreast, although at present popular, is not to be recommended, since they serve no useful purpose ; but if there is a service hatch communicating with the kitchen there should be a lamp (15-watt) above this. Another 15-watt lamp should occupy a wall bracket above the sideboard, and if a separate side table is used for carving a wall light should be situated above this also. Alternatively, the sideboard could be lit by a pair of 15- or 20-watt candle lamps.

In the Drawing- or Sitting-Room

In the drawing-room or sitting-room, the ceiling pendant with its 30-watt lamp could be supplemented by two 15-watt bracket lamps on the chimneybreast or overmantel. Of course, shades must be used so that the electric filament is not directly visible — opaque glass or parchment are generally best—and the lamps should not be stronger than 15-watt because, although a light above the fireplace is pleasant and comfortable, it is not good to have a strong light in one's face when seated at the fireside. The real illumination should come from other parts of the room. There should also be at least one floor standard and one table standard, each with 25-watt lamps.

Standard Lamps—Their Use

The advantage of standard lamps is that they may be moved about the room. Two portable standard lamps can be as useful as half-a-dozen wall brackets which are fixtures. They can be moved from bureau to bookcase, or from beside the easy chair to needlework table or gramophone, or wherever they may be required.

Of course, two or three " points " where the standard lamps may be plugged in must be fitted in the skirting board of the room, and there must be sufficient length of flex to allow of the standards being moved about.

In the Bedroom

The most important auxiliary lamp in the bedroom is one for the bedside. This may take the form of a small table standard on the bedside cabinet, or it may be designed for fixing to the bedhead. This should make an excellent light by which to read in bed, and for this purpose

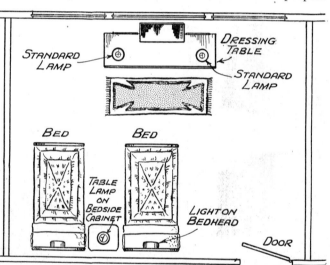

Fig. 11.—Positions for Occasional Lamps in the Bedroom.

it should be fitted with a 25-watt lamp. If reading after retiring is not contemplated a 15-watt lamp should suffice. There should also be a pair of table standards on the dressing-table.

Kitchen

The kitchen, being the place where dinner is prepared, should have a good light. A 30- or 40-watt lamp should occupy the centre of the room, above the kitchen table. There should also be a 15-watt lamp over the cooking stove and a 25-watt lamp above the sink—especially if this is in a corner of the room or in a separate scullery.

Fig. 12.—SATISFACTORY LOUNGE LIGHTING.
By means of electric wall brackets and a floor standard (Times Furnishing Co., Ltd.).

opaque glass is often used, and there are several translucent compositions showing delicate colours, some having a lustre resembling mother-of-pearl. With many of the bowl or vase-shaped table lamps now fashionable a conical shade of pleated paper or parchment is frequently used. Sometimes the paper is in wavy bands of harmonising colour or in simple patterns. Nickel and mirror glass, too, are materials which are being used for the newest table standards.

Modernising Old-Fashioned Fittings

The simplest way to modernise an electric fitting which has grown old-fashioned, or which no longer harmonises with a room which has been redecorated and refurnished, is to fit it with a new lamp shade. In floor and table standards, for example, there are turned columnar and baluster shapes which, being modelled on accepted period

Fig. 13.—MODERNISTIC LIGHTING FITTINGS.

An electric tubular table lamp.

Those described are the most important points at which lights should be situated, and the most suitable sizes for lamps, in the ordinary middle-class house.

Lamp-shade Materials for Attractive Effects and Efficient Lighting

The best materials for lamp shades are silk and parchment. For wall lights and pendants

Fig. 14.—ANOTHER MODERNISTIC TABLE LAMP.

This is in brass and aluminium with a parchment shade sprayed and stippled to match. (Best & Lloyd, Ltd.)

styles, remain in fashion almost indefinitely. It is only the lamp shade itself that is liable to grow out-moded.

Fussiness is Out-of-Date

Anything in the nature of fussiness is now old-fashioned. Ornate curvilinear shapes, gathered and pleated silk, festooning, fringes, tassels and ornamental drops—

Fig. 15 *(below)*.—SUCCESSFUL COMBINATION OF THE OLD AND THE NEW.

A modern-style electric pendant used effectively in an 18th century style dining-room. The shade has a natural-colour parchment band round the sides, an obscured rimpled bottom glass, and an opal dust cover at the top (Hope's and Best & Lloyd, Ltd.).

*Fig.*16.—HANDSOME GAS "CANDLE" PENDANT FOR A DINING-ROOM.

shades with these characteristics may make a room look rather frumpish. At present neatness and simplicity are most admired, and if your shades are too elaborate, they should be discarded in favour of plain or pleated parchment or silk, which is pleated quite simply.

CELLULOSE PAINTING OF FURNITURE

Fig. 1.—MATERIALS REQUIRED FOR CELLULOSE LACQUERING.

CELLULOSE is more in the nature of a lacquer than a paint or enamel, and for use in the home has many advantages. It dries and becomes hard, usually, in less than two hours, and leaves a beautifully smooth surface that will stand a considerable amount of wear and does not easily show marks or scratches. Cellulose finish can be applied to metal as well as wood and other materials ; it is suitable for floors and tables, iron bedsteads and tin trays, earthenware pots and cane baskets; in fact, for anything to which paint or varnish can be applied.

Possibilities

There are considerable possibilities in every home for the use of cellulose lacquer, apart from the larger pieces of furniture. The small adjuncts that help in the general decorative scheme, the table decorations, the small ornaments, and the many objects that are necessary to the general comfort. It is also possible to carry the use of the material into the kitchen, for the table top of plain deal can, for example be coated with a hard-wearing white surface that hot water cannot injure. The bread-tin, the buckets, and the

tin receptacles so necessary, can be protected from rust by one or two coats of the lacquer.

There are a number of different brands of cellulose lacquer, under various trade names, obtainable in the shops, and these are available in a large range of brilliant colours. Considering the covering properties and the lasting qualities of the material, cellulose is less expensive than paint in the long run. Quite a considerable amount of work can be done with a small can ; little more is needed, as will be seen in Fig. 1. The finish is easily applied, but care must be taken to prepare the surface, especially if previously painted articles are to be lacquered.

Preparing the Surface

The first essential in using cellulose finish is to thoroughly prepare the surface and to remove entirely any paint, varnish or enamel previously applied, leaving a perfectly smooth surface free from grease or oil. The success of the finish depends on the under surface and a good result is quite impossible if the preparatory work is omitted. Previously lacquered surfaces can be coated without much cleaning, but surfaces that have contained oil or gum, other than hard-drying shellac, must be entirely removed.

Removing Old Paint, Enamel or Varnish

Oil paint, enamel and varnish can be removed with a paint remover, of which there are many effective preparations available. In the case of very hard surfaces, it may be advisable to use heat to soften the paint sufficiently. It may be necessary to use a blow-lamp; a useful heating flame for the purpose can be improvised from a Bunsen burner or an

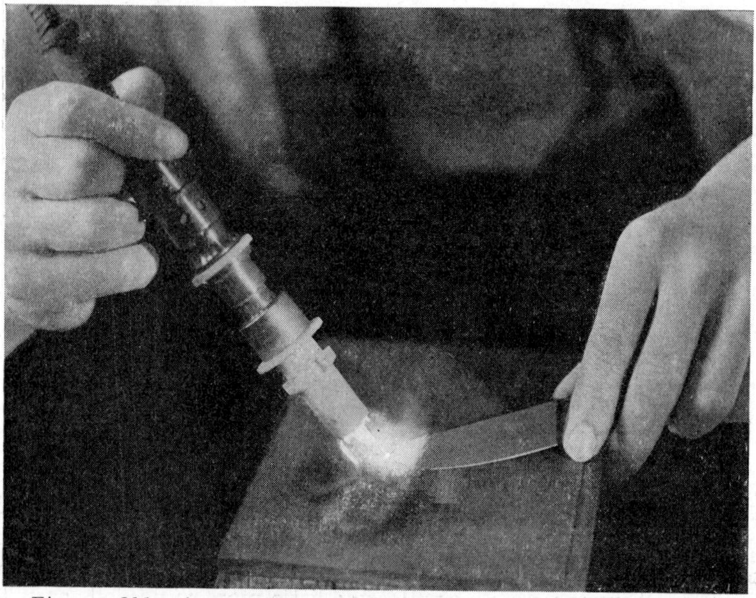

Fig. 2.—Old paint can be softened before removal with a blowpipe improvised from a Bunsen burner and an old incandescent burner.

old incandescent burner, as shown in Fig. 2. Another method, suitable for flat surfaces, is to cover the face of an electric iron with a piece of tinned sheet, and allow it to rest on the painted surface fully heated until the paint softens. Care should be taken to avoid overheating the paint, and as soon as it is soft enough, a scraper or an old knife should be used. In no case should the wood be allowed to char, for this would cause a lot of trouble in subsequent smoothing.

Cleaning up Metal Surfaces

In dealing with metal surfaces, the

frames of iron bedsteads and other forms of metal furniture, particularly those coated with a hard enamel, it is not necessary to remove the painted or enamelled surface down to the bare metal, unless the surface has been chipped. In this case heat is certainly the most effect've method of removing the old surface. Metal that has been stove enamelled cannot, however, be cleaned off in this way; the only method is to scrape it away with an old file, the final cleaning being done with emery cloth. In ordinary cases it will be sufficient to smooth the surface with emery or garnet paper, as shown in Fig. 5. This illustration shows the possibility of dealing with the cover of the electric-light switch. If the metal has been coated with lacquer, a thorough rubbing with powdered pumice or emery will do.

Using Liquid Paint Removers

Liquid paint removers are intended to soften the old paint and are generally used on painted wood surfaces. The remover must be applied liberally to the surface, either with a piece of cloth, as shown in Fig. 3, or with a brush. The softened paint should be removed with a knife or a scraper, an old kitchen knife being well suited for the purpose. Care should be taken to scrape the surface and not cut into it. Glasspaper is used finally to smooth the surface thoroughly, but should not be applied until the surface is dry.

Removing Lacquer Surfaces

Surfaces that have been previously treated with cellulose lacquer, and have

Fig. 3.—Liquid paint remover can be used to soften the old paint instead of removing by burning off, as shown in Fig. 2.

Fig. 4.—In preparing work for cellulose finish all corners should be rounded and the surface smoothed.

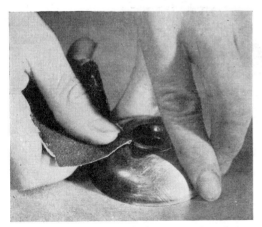

Fig. 5.—Metal surfaces should be cleaned with emery or garnet paper.

Fig. 6.—Plastic wood is used to fill up cracks or dents.

Fig. 7.—Size applied previously to the surface prevents undue absorption of the cellulose.

become chipped or otherwise damaged, can be cleaned with the special preparations sold for the purpose by the makers.

An effective remover can be made by mixing equal parts of petrol, methylated spirit and acetone. Amyl acetate can be used alone, but it is rather expensive if a large surface is to be treated.

Smooth the Surface

When all the old paint or varnish has been removed, the surface should be carefully smoothed, as shown in Fig. 4, with glasspaper or pumice powder; the latter material, if applied with a piece of thick felt, gives an excellent surface free from the scratches unavoidable with glasspaper. As cellulose does not cover well on sharp corners, these should be slightly rounded off, just enough to produce a distinct round, without spoiling the effect of the work. The idea is to produce a continuous surface without a break such as would be caused by a sharp edge.

Before applying the finish the surface should be thoroughly dusted with a clean, soft rag or, better still, washed over to remove all traces of powder. The work must be allowed to become bone dry before the lacquer is applied. The result will be very unsatisfactory if the finish is applied to a surface that is in any way damp.

Fill Up any Cracks or Dents

When the surface has been freed from paint and cleaned down, it will be possible to deal with cracks and chipped places; plastic wood will be found very useful for this purpose. This material is available in tins, as well as in tube form. It is applied with a knife and pressed well into the crack or hole, as shown in Fig. 6. As the plastic wood dries in a very few minutes, no time should be lost. Although

Fig. 8.—Do not apply cellulose finish sparingly or put a lot of pressure on the brush as shown.

it can be pared with a sharp knife and smoothed with glasspaper, when hard, just like wood, only just enough should be used and smoothed off as cleanly as possible at the time, so as to avoid unnecessary work and waste of material. If the filling is carefully done, no sign of the damaged portion will show after the lacquer has been applied, and, in addition, the surface will be quite as strong as in its original form.

Treating Absorbent Surfaces

New wood and surfaces that have an open grain or are absorbent, such as unglazed pottery, should first be filled with a paste or liquid wood filler. There are several proprietary brands available, but finely powdered whiting is as good as anything when mixed to a creamy consistency with hot, thin size. Ordinary size may be used when the wood is hard, as indicated in Fig. 7, but it is generally necessary to apply two or three coats, each one being rubbed down with pumice powder or fine glasspaper when hard. The best liquid filler is shellac, applied evenly and rubbed down ; when quite hard it leaves an excellent surface. Apart from an economical use of the cellulose finish, grain filling is advisable, because of the smoothness of the final surface.

Fig. 9.—The brush should be wiped on the edge of the tin before the finish is applied.

APPLYING THE LACQUER

The surfaces having been prepared, the lacquer should be applied as quickly as possible, and considerable care should be devoted to the choice of a brush. The best brushes are those set in rubber (see Fig. 1). The most suitable brush for cellulose is one that has long, soft bristles and at least 1 inch wide. Cheap brushes should be avoided, as the bristles are

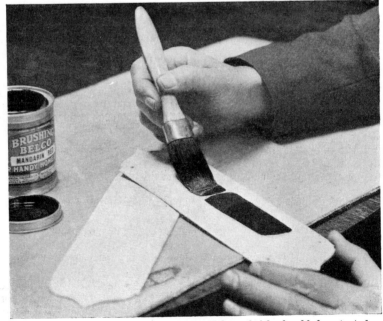

Fig. 10.—Each fresh application of cellulose finish should be started a short distance away from the end of the previous stroke.

liable to work out. As the lacquer dries so quickly, it is a difficult job to pick them out without leaving a mark. A new brush should be soaked in water for some time before use, left to dry and then thoroughly examined for loose bristles, which are liable to appear at first in the best of brushes.

Stir Cellulose Thoroughly

The cellulose should be kept away from the fire or gas flame, and the can uncovered only when the contents are being used. It must be stirred thoroughly with a wooden stick before and continually during use, in order to keep the pigment and the vehicle perfectly mixed. This is very important, as some pigments are heavy and soon sink to the bottom of the can.

Brushwork

The brush should be fully charged with lacquer by dipping it well into the liquid. The tip of the brush should be lightly wiped

Fig. 11.—Cellulose finish can be applied to picture and mirror frames without removing the glass if a protective sheet of tin or cardboard is used.

on the inner edge of the can, as shown in Fig. 9, just before it is carried to the surface. In all cases the tip should be used only, and the fibres inclined at an angle to the surface, so that a clean stroke can be made in one direction. The lacquer should be allowed to flow from the brush, and not in any way forced on the surface. When one stroke has been completed the next should be commenced a short distance away, as shown in Fig. 10, the lacquer being laid off towards the previously painted line, so that it merges with it without a definite join.

Owing to the rapidity with which cellulose finish hardens, it is necessary to carry through the work with some speed. If the lacquer works thickly it can be thinned with the special preparation provided for the purpose. Every maker supplies a special thinning fluid made to suit the finish. In order to obtain a smooth, even surface, the new strokes should be placed side by side, as well as end to end, not touching at first, but joined up with a light stroke of the brush as soon as it has been emptied.

Actually the spreading of the lacquer is the least troublesome part of using cellulose finish. The risk of failure is quite small. Given a perfectly smooth surface, properly prepared, a good brush and the material at the right consistency, it is almost impossible to go wrong.

On Vertical Surfaces

In dealing with vertical surfaces care should be taken to apply the finish sparingly. If the brush is too full the liquid will run and dry in ridges. This peculiarity is not noticeable when working on a flat surface, as the lacquer soon flows out in all directions and forms a smooth surface. Still it is not necessary to use an excess even on a flat surface. With ordinary care brush marks will not show, the only likelihood of a badly finished surface appearing is through making too many brush strokes and by working the material over the surface for a longer period than is necessary, or by a too economical use of the lacquer, as indicated in Fig. 8.

It is always advisable to tackle definite

reas and complete them. In dealing with a chair, as shown in the illustrations, the front legs, for instance, should be done first, then the under-rail and the back, and finally the seat. When once a layer of lacquer has been brushed on, the remainder of the surface should be covered. If one portion is allowed to harden, a join without a mark or a ridge is almost impossible.

Lacquering on Lacquer

When it is desired to change from a dark to a light colour on a suitable smooth surface that needs no special preparation other than the removal of grease marks and a light rub with fine glass-paper or pumice powder, it is advisable to coat the surface with an undercoat of an appropriate shade. The surface can then be completed with one or two coats of the desired colour. This applies to metal and wood surfaces. In changing from a very dark colour, black for example, to a light tint, it is a good plan to cover the surface with at least two coats of white. The light tint will be much more effective on the white ground than would be the case if the undercoat were omitted.

Obtaining Rich Gloss

A rich gloss can be obtained on the newly lacquered surface when it has become hard by rubbing it with a soft cloth. Several hours should be allowed for the cellulose to get hard enough. The result will be a beautiful soft gloss unobtainable with any other material.

Coating Frames

Cellulose finish is admirably adapted to the decoration of mirror and picture frames, and the work can be done without removing the glass if desired. In this case a sheet of tinned iron, or a piece of cardboard should be placed against the glass, as shown in Fig. 11. If possible the glass should be removed, so that the work can be done in the manner shown in

Fig. 12. Possibilities of adding to the general colour scheme by making the picture frame suit the picture may be realised quite easily through the large range of cellulose colours that are available.

Fig. 12.—The most satisfactory method of applying the finish is to remove the glass.

Taking Care of the Brushes

When the work is finished, the brush should be washed immediately with soap in hot water. The soap should be rubbed well into the bristles. Dry soap powder can be used, but ordinary soap flakes are best. The soap should be rubbed out thoroughly and the brush dried before using it again. If the lacquer has hardened on the brush, the only way of cleaning it is to place it in the special thinning preparation prepared by the makers of the particular lacquer used. The brush should be allowed to remain in the liquid for some time until the bristles are quite soft; the liquid is brushed out on an old board or a pad of newspaper and then the brush is thoroughly washed in soap and water. It is a good plan to keep clean brushes in a box or to wrap them in paper, so that contact with dust is avoided.

An Inexpensive Soiled-Linen Container

THE useful container for soiled linen shown in Fig. 1 makes an attractive article, especially if the covering matches the curtains or bedspread, or, perhaps, the loose covers of the bedroom chairs. The container is a banana box, which is easily obtainable. An alternative is a round plywood barrel in which the hypo used by photographers is packed in bulk. These can occasionally be obtained from wholesale chemists, photographic dealers and photographers.

It is not always possible to procure a perfectly sound banana box, but damaged sides can be repaired with brown paper or by using gummed tape. The box is first of all cut down to the level of the first band, as shown in Fig. 2; a fine tenon saw can be used, but a sharp knife will do. The cut edges should be smoothed with glasspaper.

Measure the height and diameter of the box and, in cutting out the covering material, allow $6\frac{1}{2}$ inches in the height and about one and a half times the diameter. Turn the material inwards, machine up the sides and then turn in first $\frac{1}{4}$ inch, and then 2 inches at the top to form the frill. Machine along the bottom and again about $\frac{1}{2}$ inch up to provide for a drawstring or elastic. The

Fig. 1.—Soiled-Linen Container made from a Banana Crate.

The covering for the container can be selected to match the bedroom curtains or bed-covers.

Fig. 1A.—The Inner Calico Bag containing the Soiled Linen is Easily Lifted Out.

bottom is turned in $\frac{1}{4}$ inch and then $\frac{1}{2}$ inch and sewn.

A child's wooden hoop, as shown in Fig. 2, is now procured; it should be the same diameter as the top of the box. Make a calico bag to the same diameter as the hoop and deep enough to fill the box. The top of the bag is sewn to the ring, which will rest on the top of the box and hold it in position.

The top of the box is made from a piece of plywood cut to the same diameter as the outside of the hoop. The outside edges should be slightly rounded off with glasspaper to leave them perfectly smooth. Place the top on the cretonne, or whatever material is used for the covering, cutting it from 3 inches to 4 inches larger all round. A strong draw-thread is now sewn along the outside edge and pulled up tight, as shown in Fig. 3. Before the string is tied, a handle is made from a folded strip of the material and sewn to the centre. Some bradawl holes bored through the wood will enable the handle to be much more securely attached. A calico lining is made by cutting the material a little larger than the diameter of the lid, the edges being turned in neatly and sewn to the cretonne.

Three ordinary drawer knobs form the feet.

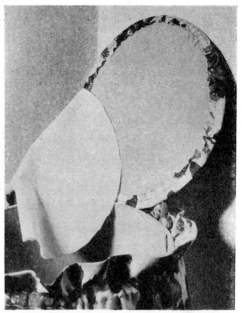

Fig. 2.—PARTS OF THE CONTAINER.

A banana box, two bags, a small hoop, three drawer knobs and some plywood, is practically all that is necessary.

Fig. 3.—MAKING UP THE CONTAINER.

The lid is covered and lined, and the crate is enclosed in the covering bag, which is drawn tight at the top, as shown.

Fig. 4.—THREE DRAWER KNOBS, FIXED UNDERNEATH THE WOODEN FRAMING, FORM THE FEET.
Note how covering is drawn in at the bottom.

GOOD AND BAD POURERS

Fig. 1.—A METAL TEA-POT HARDLY EVER DRIPS.

By noting the shape of the spout the clue is found to the secret of choosing pots and jugs that will pour well, without dripping on to the table-cloth. The china tea-pot here is the nearest approach to the metal one. Its spout projects sharply, but could not be thinner at the tip without chipping.

Fig. 2.—Note also the sharply projecting spouts of both these jugs. Jugs like this can always be depended on to pour smoothly without drips when stood **up.**

Fig. 3.—Compare these drooping, thick-edged lips with the good pourers seen in the previous illustrations. All these examples drip.

BEAUTY CULTURE

MANICURE AND CARE OF THE SKIN

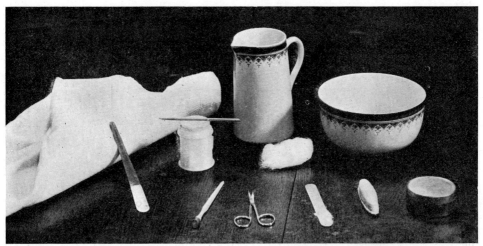

*Fig. 1.—*MANICURE REQUISITES.
Reading from left to right—towel, steel file, peroxide and orange stick, hoofstick, cuticle scissors,
jug of hot soapy water, cotton-wool, emery board, bowl, buffer and nail polish.

THIS article on the care of the hands and skin is the second of the series on the subject of beauty culture. A later section will deal with the care of the hair and simple home hairdressing.

MANICURE

Materials Required:—

Place a comfortable chair in a good light with the following articles (*see* Fig. 1) close to hand :—

Flexible steel file, about 7 inches long.
Small shallow bowl.
Jug containing about a pint of very hot soapy water.
Orange stick with the end filed to a rounded point.
Small utensil containing a little peroxide of hydrogen.
A small piece of best quality cotton-wool.
Soft face towel.
Rubber-ended hoofstick.
Pair of fine curved cuticle scissors.
Emery board.
Nail polish.
Buffer.

First Operation—Filing

First the nails must be filed. Hold the steel file between the thumb and fingers of the right hand, fingers uppermost, as in Fig. 2. Start with the little finger of the right hand. Place the edge of the file under the nail at the inner corner, so that the file is nearly parallel with the nail (Fig. 3). Draw it with a light, quick movement along the edge of the nail to the centre, using the whole length of the file. Replace it at the outer corner, drawing it back to the centre with a similar movement. Repeat the movement until the nail is the same length and shape as the finger-tip. File the other fingers and thumb in order in the same way.

The Second Operation—Soaking

Pour a little of the soapy water into the bowl and immerse the fingers and thumb of the left hand until the cuticle is thoroughly softened. Dry the fingers.

Then Apply Peroxide

Moisten the pointed end of the orange stick (the pointing can be done on an

7—2

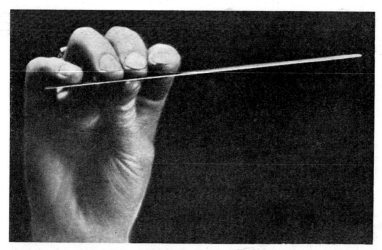

Fig. 2.—How to Hold the File.

the same order. With the emery board tidy the edges of the nails, leaving them smooth. The emery board may be used backwards and forwards, and even across the edge of the nail, as long as the surface of the nail is not marked.

Take the cuticle scissors and carefully snip off any loosened cuticle or skin still adhering.

emery board) and wrap round it a fragment of cotton-wool. Dip it in the peroxide and, starting with the little finger, work round the cuticle, pressing it down gently but firmly. Then pass the padded stick under the nail, gently removing any dirt. On no account use any force. Wipe off the peroxide quickly with the towel. Repeat the process on the other fingers and the thumb.

Soak the right hand and treat in the same way, then wash both hands and dry thoroughly, pressing down the cuticle, Massage in the lotion usually used after washing and dust with boracic. The nails are now ready for polishing.

Remove Loosened Cuticle

With the rubber-ended hoofstick work the loosened skin off the nail, pressing down the cuticle, taking the fingers in

Polishing

It is best to use a paste, of which there are several excellent makes on the market. Apply a little to each nail and polish with the buffer, rubbing briskly. A polishing stone or powder can be used instead, but these are apt to harden the cuticles and make the nails brittle. A liquid polish has the same effect, but if this is used apply as follows:— Dip the brush supplied in the polish, wipe off some on the lip of the bottle, and make two quick vertical strokes from the edge of the half-moon up the nail. The half-moon must be left free from polish (Fig. 8).

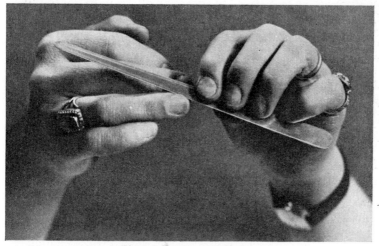

Fig. 3.—Filing the Nails.
Note the angle of the file in relation to the nail.

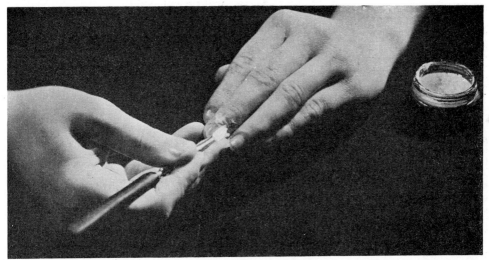

Fig. 4.—Pressing Back the Cuticle.

This shows a metal instrument being used with cuticle cream. Readers may prefer to use the hoofstick and cotton-wool soaked with peroxide for pressing back the cuticle, as recommended in the article, especially as the metal instrument needs skilled handling to prevent damage to the nails.

A weekly manicure should be sufficient if the directions relating to the daily care of the hands are followed. The nails should be rubbed each day with the buffer, fresh polish being applied as necessary.

ERRORS TO BE AVOIDED

Filing

The steel file must only be used as directed and not rubbed backward and forward with a sawing movement

Fig. 5.—Cleaning the Nails.

After pressing back cuticle, insert the small pad of cotton-wool soaked with peroxide under the nail at the point of the orange stick and remove any dirt.

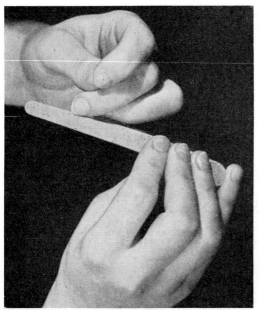

Fig. 6.—TIDY THE EDGES OF THE NAILS
WITH EMERY BOARD.

Fig. 7.—POLISHING THE NAILS.
The buffer is used after paste or dry polish
has been applied to the nails—but not after liquid
polish. The above picture is a good example of
how not to use the buffer. It is rubbing the fingers
as well as the nail, and also the third and little
finger nails are hardly being touched by the buffer.

which will split the nail. Neither
must it be drawn across the edge of
the nail. (*See* Fig. 3.)

Using the Orange Stick

This must on no account be forced
down the nail below its junction
with the finger, or permanent injury
will result. All the work with the
stick should be very gentle or the nail
will be damaged. If peroxide is left
on too long white marks will appear on
the skin.

Using Cuticle Scissors

The danger here is of cutting too
deeply, and leaving raw places, or even
drawing blood. Only the loosened skin
should be cut. The cuticle proper
must never be cut, as cutting thickens
it. Cuticle that has been neglected
cannot be put right in one manicure.

How to Clean Off Polish

If a liquid polish has previously
been used and some still remains on
the nail, before starting to file, clean
this off with a little alcohol or peroxide,
rubbing gently until no trace of the
polish or peroxide remains.

The Tools

The tools enumerated among the
requisites are all that are needed.
Metal tools should not be used by the
amateur, as the risk is too great. The
tools provided in most manicure sets,
even expensive ones, are of very little
practical use. Those mentioned here
can be purchased at any of the large
stores or chemists at a reasonable
price.

CURE OF UNHEALTHY
CONDITIONS OF THE HANDS

Chapped Hands

Soak the hands well at night in hot
soapy water, to which has been added a
little salad oil, gently massaging them
the while. Dab them with a soft absorbent towel until dry. Coat generously
with the glycerine, almond oil and

oatmeal mixture (*see* page 21). Put on white cotton gloves which have a slit in the palms and a small hole in the tips of the fingers and thumbs for ventilation.

Ridged Nails

The ridging is caused by a lack of lime in the system or too much acid in the blood. A doctor should be consulted. A ridged nail will split very easily.

Split Nail

Do not try to file below the split, but cut a piece of adhesive tape just large enough to hold the torn nail together, adjust it carefully over the tear, and apply liquid nail polish very evenly over the nail and plaster. When dry make a second application. Nails that are liable to split may be massaged nightly with a little warm olive oil.

White Spots on Nails

White spots may be caused by using the orange stick too heavily. To cure these, make a paste of equal parts of myrrh and turpentine and apply this every night. Remove it in the morning with warm olive oil.

Bitten Finger Nails

This habit may have been induced by the discomfort caused by the cuticle having been allowed to grow up over the nail. Correct this and keep the nails well coated with liquid polish during the day and wear gloves at night till the habit has been thoroughly broken.

Chilblains

Chilblains are caused by a lack of calcium in the blood. A doctor should be consulted. A course of sunlight treatment before the cold weather sets in has been found very beneficial. Chilblains on the fingers just below the cuticle will badly scar and dent the new nail as it grows up. To alleviate the pain and discomfort of chilblains soak the hands at night in

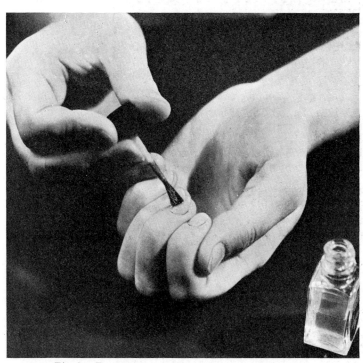

Fig. 8.—Polishing the Nails with Liquid Polish.
Make two quick vertical strokes of the brush from the edge of the half moon up the nail. Do not cover the half moon with the liquid.

very hot mustard and water for half an hour, dab gently with a soft towel until dry, and massage tallow well in. This can usually be obtained at any plumbing and ironmongery business. Wear gloves during the night. Never warm the hands in front of the fire, but grease them, wash in hot water, dry carefully, and lightly powder with boracic.

Hot Hands

This is a trouble due to a constitutional weakness and is not easy to cure. The following lotion will greatly help to alleviate the trouble:—Glycerine, 2 ozs.; sal-volatile, 2 ozs.; red lotion, ½ oz. It should be applied after washing and will keep the skin smooth, as well as cool the hands. The slight clammy feeling it leaves may be removed by the use of a little dusting powder.

THE CARE OF THE HANDS

This is an important item in the daily toilet, regular attention being much more satisfactory than occasional violent and expensive manicures. After the evening bath rub cold cream well into the hands and wipe off the superfluous cream. Then using the tip of the thumb work a little vaseline in round the cuticles, pressing them down. After the morning wash rub into the hands a little glycerine and elderflower water, again pressing the cuticle gently down. Then dust over the hands a little boracic powder and work it in until the clammy feeling occasioned by the glycerine is removed. There are some skins that glycerine does not suit, in which case liquid paraffin (medicinal) may be used instead.

Household Tasks and the Hands

To protect the hands while doing household duties it is a good plan to wear gloves.

Avoid the use of soda or powdered soap, both of which are most injurious to the skin and are largely the cause of chapped hands and cracked finger-tips. Soapflakes are a good substitute. Cleaning powders containing soda should be avoided.

Keep a small piece of flannel handy, and when scouring saucepans with a metal pot-cleaner, put it over the top of the cleaner so that the finger-nails are protected from being scratched by the cleaner.

CARE OF THE SKIN

For the purposes of this article it is unnecessary to describe the construction of the skin in detail. The function of the *sweat glands* is to pour out fluid on to the skin. The fluid, by evaporating, cools the skin and is of value in regulating the temperature of the body. The amount of water lost by invisible perspiration is from 1½ to 2 pints daily.

Proper Cleansing of the Skin

The sweat glands open on to the outer skin in the form of pores. In order that these glands may function properly it is necessary that these openings should be kept free from dirt. It is obvious that during the day dust and dirt accumulate on the surface of the skin and are even pressed into the pores. This dirt must be removed whenever possible before retiring to bed, the ideal method being, of course a warm bath.

The Evening Bath

It is not desirable to use a highly-scented soap, as the scent acts as an irritant to the skin. The best to use is white Castile. To prevent chapping, dust with the following powder:—Equal parts of fuller's earth, zinc oxide and boracic.

The Morning Bath or Sponge Down

A sponge down each morning, either with tepid water or hot water, followed by a cold sponge, will stimulate the skin so that it will function properly.

SLOW COMBUSTION BOILERS
HOW TO USE THEM TO THE BEST ADVANTAGE

THERE are two essentially different types of boilers. Perhaps the best known is what is commonly called the "domestic" type. This is used for the purpose of providing a supply of hot water, through a circulating system, for bath and general purposes in the home. The other type is the "heating" type, which is used to heat water in a circulating system of pipes and radiators, for the purpose of warming a house or certain rooms.

Fig. 1.—CLEANING THE GRATE.

The fire should be poked periodically at the grate level so as to sift out the ashes and prevent the formation of clinker. With anthracite fuel poking should be infrequent.

the hand holes provided. This cleaning is specially necessary in districts where the water is "hard." For example, London is mostly supplied with water which comes from districts having a chalky subsoil, with the result that, when the water is heated, lime or what is usually called "furr" is deposited in the boiler.

The Temperature of the Water

More lime is deposited if the temperature to which the water is heated is high. It is, therefore, best to keep the temperature down to a reasonable figure, such as 140° F., which is hot enough for domestic purposes, as a very hot bath is only about 110° F. Under ordinary home conditions, cleaning out requires to be done about once a year, and it is, of course, a job for the plumber.

DOMESTIC BOILERS

A typical domestic boiler is the "Ideal," shown in Fig. 2. Such a type is more economical than the old-fashioned block boiler, which is fitted at the back of the kitchener. With the modern independent domestic boiler, the fire is enclosed by the boiler, or, putting it another way, the boiler is the fireplace and not merely a part of it.

Boilers Must be Cleaned Occasionally

Domestic boilers should be made with a reasonably large waterway and must be so shaped that every part of the waterway can be cleaned periodically through

A Fire for Cooking as Well

Another kind of domestic boiler is made circular (as in Fig. 5), so that the fire is entirely enclosed by the water jacket. It is rather more efficient, but boilers like that shown in Fig. 2 are more popular, not only because they are made smaller and cheaper, but because the fire can be

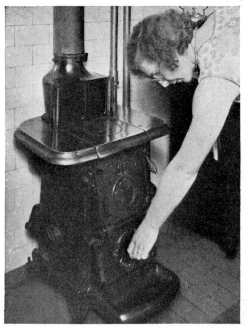

Fig. 2.—OPENING THE BOTTOM DAMPER
TO INCREASE THE DRAUGHT.

Fig. 4.—REMOVE THE ASHES
DAILY.

This has the effect of supplying more air to the fire, which consequently burns fiercer. A hotter water supply is then, of course, the result, provided fuelling is correctly attended to.

This is important, not only to ensure a sufficient supply of air to the fire, but also to prevent overheating of the grate bars. Removal of the ashes is a very easy matter, as can be seen above.

Fig. 3.—CHECKING THE DRAUGHT FOR SLOW
OR NIGHT RUNNING ON A DOMESTIC BOILER.

Fig. 3A.—CHECKING THE DRAUGHT FOR SLOW
RUNNING ON A HEATING BOILER.

opened up and, in fact, used for a certain amount of cooking (*see* Fig. 12).

Water which Rusts Boiler Metal

Although most of the domestic boilers on the market are made of cast iron, some are made of welded steel plate, while boilers of copper are available for use in soft-water districts. Where the water comes from a peaty subsoil it is " soft," that is, practically no lime is present, but, unfortunately, such water has a corrosive or rusting influence on ordinary iron or steel.

Rusting and its Prevention

The discoloration of the water by rusting can be prevented if the iron boilers are used in a rustless finish, and this is preferable to using boilers made of copper, as the latter are rather expensive. Most makes of domestic boilers are made in both ordinary and rustless finishes.

HEATING BOILERS

Waterways Need No Cleaning

With the heating type of boiler the conditions are different. The same water is circulated through the system for months, or even years ; therefore, there is no need for the boiler to have large waterways, or to provide for them to be cleaned out. As the water need not be changed, there is no need to worry as to whether it is hard or soft.

When the Boiler is not in Use

It is, however, very important to see that the heating boiler is left clean and free from soot and ashes during the summer period when it is out of use. Few people realise that the idle season is responsible for practically all the wear which a boiler suffers, except, of course, such minor parts.as grate bars.

The presence of soot on the water-backed surface of the metal, or of ashes or half-burnt fuel in the firebox would

Fig. 5.—ANOTHER TYPE OF DOMESTIC BOILER.

scarcely affect the durability of the metal if it could be kept perfectly dry. This condition takes care of itself while the boiler is in use, but, unfortunately, it is well-nigh impossible to prevent a certain amount of moisture when it is out of use, owing to the humidity of the atmosphere condensing on the cold metal. The remedy, therefore, is to keep the metal clean, as the dampness alone has only negligibly harmful effect. It is the combination of sulphurous matter and dampness which does the damage. It will be seen that these remarks apply almost entirely to the heating type of boiler, as the domestic boiler is in use all the year round.

If the doors of the boiler are left open, the metal will be kept as dry as possible by the slight draught up the chimney.

FUELS AND FUELLING

Fuels to Use

Either coke or anthracite coal can be used, as they are smokeless. While anthracite is rather expensive, it has the advantage of being labour saving. Not only is it cleaner because there is much less ash in it, but it is much heavier, and a charge or scuttle will, therefore, last a longer time.

Avoid Ordinary Coal

Ordinary house coal is inadvisable and, in fact, dangerous, owing to its gaseous nature. Although it could be used with the domestic type when opened up, as in an ordinary fire grate, house coal burned in a closed boiler is certain to cause an accumulation of gas, which may explode with dire results.

Select the Right Size of Fuel

The coke or anthracite should be the correct size for the boiler. This is very important, as when the fuel is too large, or too small, the fire is likely to go out. The proper sizing of fuel is important for securing the stabilised conditions of draught which are essential if a boiler is to be run with a minimum amount of attention and for long periods.

Hot Water First Thing Without Trouble

Heating boilers are run continuously day and night, and the domestic

Fig. 6.—If a heating boiler is fitted with an "indirect" cylinder, it can also be used to supply hot water.

type should preferably run in the same way, as thereby a supply of hot water is available first thing in the morning. The alternative is letting the fire out each evening and putting one's self to the trouble of re-lighting the fire each morning. If proper attention is given to buying fuel of suitable size, and most merchants now know the size required for the various sizes and makes of boilers on the market, and provided the grate is kept clear and the dampers adjusted to slow running, as later described, no difficulty will be experienced in keeping the fire alight. Continuous running not only saves a lot of work, but is little or no more expensive than the other method.

Trying Out Other Fuels in Your Boiler

Besides ordinary gas coke, which is now generally broken down and sold in definite sizes identified either by a name or number, and anthracite

coal, which is always sold in certain sizes, other fuels are now offered to the public under fancy names. Care must be exercised in buying these patent fuels, to see that they are really suitable for the boiler. It is better to buy a sample bag first. The chief points to notice in the experiment are the amount of ash and clinker left, how long the bag as well as a single charge lasts, and whether the fire is easily controlled.

How and When to Poke the Fire

Speaking of clinker, it should be known that clinker is merely the ash which has become fused into a mass. This happens when the fire is not regularly cleared of ashes. Of course a good deal of the ash falls through the grate into the ash-box underneath, but the fire requires periodic poking at the grate level, not only to allow the air to get through, but to prevent the making of clinker. When anthracite is used, the poking should be kept to a minimum, as not only is there less ash to contend with, but the poking will cause the loss of good fuel through the bars, owing to the fact that anthracite breaks up into quite small pieces while burning (see Fig. 1).

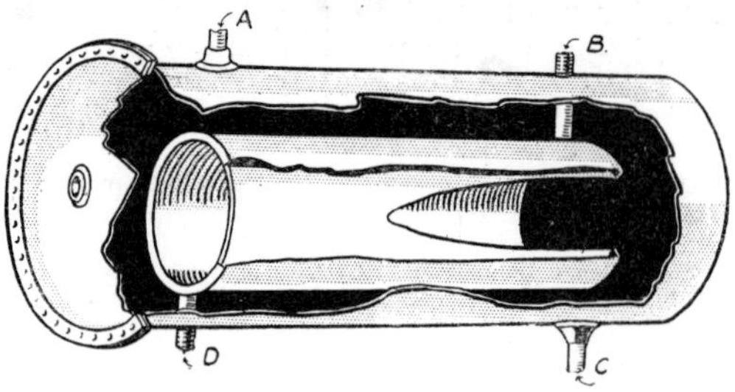

Fig. 6A.—An "Indirect" Cylinder.

Hot water from the heating boiler enters at A and goes out back to the boiler at C. Cold water from the cistern enters the jacketed cylinder at B and goes out at D. The boiler water thus heats the cold water. See also Fig. 6.

GETTING PROPER DRAUGHT

What Does the Flue Do?

A good draught is easily controlled, but a poor draught will cause more trouble than any other condition associated with slow combustion boilers. Yet it is true that, in nine cases out of ten, poor draught would have been avoided if attention had been paid in the first instance to the proper fixing of the boiler to the chimney flue. The true function of a flue is not always understood. Without entering into technicalities, it may be said that all fuel requires a certain amount of air mixed with it, if good combustion is to be secured. Each single pound weight of fuel to be properly burned needs over ten pounds weight of air mixed with it, and the problem is to get an adequate air supply. It is not really a problem,

Fig. 7.—HEATING BOILER FITTED WITH AUTOMATIC DAMPER REGULATOR.

This automatically regulates the supply of air to the fire and so controls the temperature of the water.

as any ordinary chimney flue will suffice. The points to notice, however, are the following: The connection between the smoke outlet of boiler and the brick flue must be airtight. It should be as short as possible and provided with a removable cover, either in the pipe or elbow if one is needed, in order to facilitate cleaning. The flue should be an independent one for the boiler alone, and no other fire-places should lead into it.

Fitting Boiler to an Existing Flue

Probably most cases of poor draught occur where a boiler is connected to a flue which was previously built for some other purpose, as for example, a kitchen range. It is not sufficient merely to connect the boiler outlet to the base of such a flue and close off the opening with a sheet of metal. Such a method means that the smoke, or products of combustion, leaving the boiler at a certain velocity will lose that velocity in the larger space at the bottom of the brick flue. The right method is to continue the boiler connection up to that point when the brick flue assumes its normal size; thus the velocity is maintained and a good draught will result. The fitting of a boiler is not, of course, the responsibility of the house-wife, but she is the sufferer when bad work is done, and this information is only given in order to explain what usually causes bad draught.

Methods of Controlling the Fire by Dampers

Every boiler is provided with certain dampers for the control of the draught, and therefore the amount of fuel to be burned. Air admitted underneath the fire will help combustion, and air admitted above the fire will hinder it, the latter

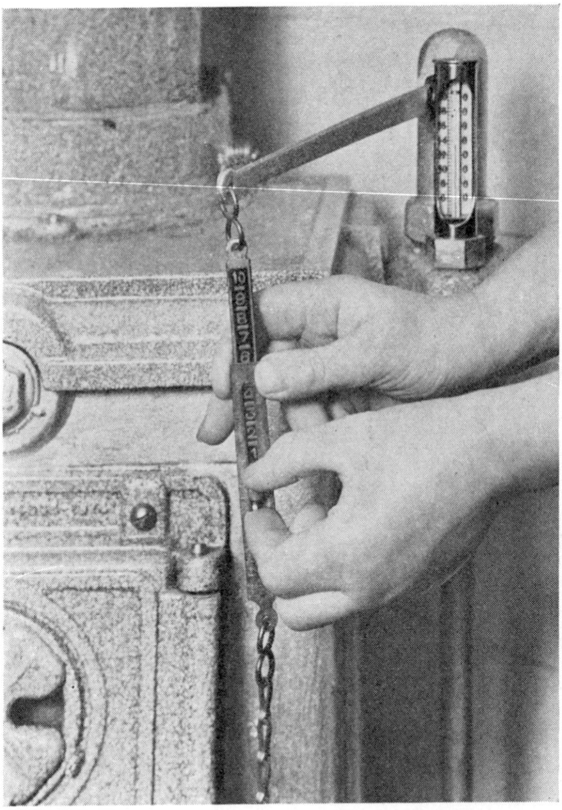

Fig. 8.—ADJUSTING THE SETTING OF THE DAMPER REGULATOR.

The higher the regulator is set, the greater will be the opening of the damper, as seen in Fig. 8a. This will have the effect of making the fire burn more fiercely, and heat the water to a higher temperature.

for the simple reason that the chimney temperature would become cooled down more or less, and as a hot flue makes draught, any cold air entering the flue must check the fire. Another method of checking the fire is to use some kind of damper by means of which the area of smoke outlet can be reduced, although it should be stated that, with some boilers,

both these methods of checking are provided. It is difficult to describe these dampers in detail, as they vary in design with the various makes of boilers, some castings being hinged, some turning on a spindle, while others may be a sliding type. Sometimes the ashpit door is made to slide along, and then a separate draught damper is unnecessary. However, the shape or pattern of the damper matters little if their purpose is understood.

Adjusting the Dampers for Day and Night Operation

By the suitable adjustment of the several dampers, a boiler can be run fast or slow, according to the needs of the day. For night running, the ashpit damper may require to be almost closed, but trial and error for the first week is the only way to determine the best adjustment of dampers for a particular boiler, as no two chimney flues are alike. Once the proper adjustments have been noted, however, the conditions should remain constant, except, perhaps, when a high wind is blowing, always provided the same size fuel is used and the grate kept reasonably clear of ashes. If trouble is experienced in keeping the fire in, note whether the fire has gone out or burned out. If practically all of the fuel has been burned, then the damper should be set for still slower operation. If the fire has gone out and most of the fuel remains unburnt, then rather more draught is obviously needed. Whether the ashpit damper should then be opened wider, or the draught checked a little less by smokehood damper or dampers is a matter for experiment.

Automatic Control of the Water Temperature

Much time and trouble can be saved by having some type of automatic damper regulator fitted to the boiler. Fig. 7 shows a heating boiler fitted with such a regulator controlling only the fresh-air supply to the fire, and not the smoke-hood dampers, which are readily set by hand and do not need continual adjustment. This method is quite sufficient in most cases, as a constant water temperature is assured by merely regulating the air intake to the fire.

The close-up view of regulator, Fig. 8, shows the brass adjusting fitting which enables the water temperature to be varied at will. When set at, say, No. 6, experience may show that the ashpit damper is closed tight when the thermometer records a temperature of 120° F.

Alternatively, a setting of " 8," which, of course, means that the chain has been shortened, will serve to keep the ashpit damper open, as in Fig. 8A, for a longer period of time, and a water temperature of perhaps 140° F. will be automatically maintained.

It is a simple matter to make a few tests and see what setting of the adjusting fitting gives the various temperatures between the ordinary limit of working, say, 120° F. to 180° F. It will be realised that whereas 120° F. may suffice on a mild day, a damp, cold day may make a temperature of 160° necessary.

LIGHTING THE FIRE

Although it has already been stressed that it is preferable to keep the fire burning day and night, something might now be said about lighting the fire. The grate should be cleared of any remains of a previous fire and the ashpit cleared of ashes. Throw in a number of balls of newspaper and then some dry, thin sticks of wood, followed by thicker pieces. After seeing that the dampers are properly set for quick firing, light the paper and allow the fire to get well alight and the chimney hot before putting on a couple or more shovels of coke and other fuel. The ashpit damper should not be too wide open, otherwise the wood will burn out before the coke is well ignited.

It Won't Go Out if You Do This

Economy in the use of wood will be effected if, at the beginning of operations, the back half of the grate is covered with a small quantity of coke. This will reduce the free air space of the grate temporarily, and is an almost certain cure for the fire going out. Where, for some reason, the draught is habitually sluggish, a small

Fig. 8A.—SHOWING ASHPIT DAMPER OPENED BY MEANS OF REGULATOR.

When the temperature of the water has reached the point required the damper automatically closes and regulates the fire to the intensity which will maintain the water at this temperature.

amount of house coal may have to be used for the first small charge. A larger quantity of fuel should be added as soon as the fire is well alight and the dampers then re-set according to requirements. Remember, a steady, slow fire is more economical than where it is run with extremes of draught. This latter is usually evidence of a lack of method and is wasteful.

*Fig. 9.—*Emptying the Boiler.
Take the flexible pipe to an outside drain.

*Fig. 10.—*Easy Method of Stoking
Fire.

*Fig. 11.—*Opening up Boiler Front to
Obtain Full Open Fire.

*Fig. 12.—*Boiler fire may be used when there
is a little extra cooking to be done.

A convenient and clean device for lighting the fire is the gas-poker, which can be purchased at most ironmongers. This is linked up to a nearby gas point by means of a flexible gas pipe. After lighting the poker, it is placed at the bottom of the stove. The fire is then made up with fresh fuel to a depth of about 6 inches. The damper and front doors of the fire should, in this case, be left open until the fuel is well alight. Afterwards, the poker is withdrawn and the front and ashpit drawers are shut.

Kitchen refuse, the contents of the sink tidy, paper and garden and vegetable refuse can readily be burnt in the boiler fire provided a good glowing fire has previously been obtained.

GENERAL RUNNING HINTS

Removing Ashes

Care should be taken to see that the ashes are removed daily. Not only is this necessary to ensure an adequate supply of air to the fire, but, if the ashes pile up in the ashpit, there is a danger of the grate bars burning out. It is only because these castings are air-cooled that they do not become red-hot and warp out of shape. If a quantity of ash or clinker remains on the top of the grate, the same overheating will occur (see Fig. 4).

A Harmful Way of Brightening the Fire

On no account should the clinker door, or other door above the grate level, be opened as a means of brightening the fire. This is a lazy way of stoking a boiler, and although effective to a certain extent, must lead to trouble. Clinker is also unnecessarily made in this way.

In Frosty Weather

In frosty weather the fire should certainly be kept running, to avoid any risk of the water in the installation freezing.

Leaving the House Vacant

Should the house be left unoccupied during the winter months, it is better for the water to be run off. Alternatively never re-light the fire in frosty weather without first seeing that the pipes are free from ice. If water runs freely from the draw-off cock on the boiler, it can generally be assumed there is no danger. To meet these conditions, it is a good practice to fit a safety valve on the boiler.

Fit a Thermometer

Every boiler should have a thermometer ; otherwise the setting of dampers must be done rather blindly. The knowledge that a given water temperature is secured with a certain arrangement of dampers makes the work of stoking easier and assures satisfactory running with a minimum of fuel.

Fitting a Radiator on a Domestic Boiler

When a small domestic boiler is fitted with the idea of assuring a constant supply of hot water, it is worth while considering the fixing of a radiator, say, in the hall or the living room. It is very unlikely that the full power of the boiler will be wanted for hot water all day long, therefore the surplus might just as well be used to provide a certain amount of warmth.

Adapting a Heating Boiler for Supplying Hot Water

Although it has been stated earlier that a heating boiler is generally made with small waterways and without provision for cleaning out lime deposit, it does not follow that it cannot be used for domestic hot-water supply, as well as heating radiators. If what is called an indirect cylinder, as shown in Fig. 6, is used, then the water which circulates through the heating boiler and the radiators also passes through a heater or coil which is fixed inside the indirect cylinder. Thus the storage water in the cylinder is heated by the water which circulates through the heater portion of the cylinder, without any mixing of water.

STORAGE AND CARE OF GRAMOPHONE RECORDS

Fig. 1.—A CONVENIENT METHOD OF STORING RECORDS.

Shelves on either side of the chimneybreast holding the records, either singly or, better still, in albums. It should be noted that the correct way to store the records is to fill each partitioned space and *not* to allow them to rest at an angle.

The Gramophone Library

FOR the proper enjoyment of a gramophone a reasonably extensive collection of records is essential. A gramophone with a repertoire of only six or a dozen discs would be wretchedly dull ; and probably the smallest gramophone library which anyone should possess who hopes for lasting pleasure from their instrument would amount to fifty discs. Of course, if one is purchasing a gramophone for the first time, there would be no objection to starting with less—say twelve records as a minimum. But the collection must grow. You must add at least one new disc to your shelves every week. Then, in the course of a year, you will have added fifty records. In two or three years you will have collected a real library of gramophone music.

Which Records Shall I Buy?

Now records are expensive. Even supposing that you confine yourself to the standard 10-inch discs and 12-inch discs (and much of the finest music in existence is now available in these discs), it still cannot be said that good records are at all low in price. There are, it is true, cheaper kinds which may be had for so little as 1s. 3d. each. But one's purchases in this class are best restricted to ephemeral dance music, of a kind which quickly passes out of fashion.

A Good Record Represents Capital Invested

All good records are worth careful storing. They are not only more costly ; they embody music of permanent appeal, music, in most instances, which will be as highly esteemed fifty years hence as it is to-day. The price of the record is, therefore, capital invested in future pleasure, and for every reason the record should be treated with the utmost care.

Don't Keep Records Like a Pack of Cards

The first thing one should never do is to leave one's records lying about. The *worst* way of keeping them is to stack them in an untidy pile covered only by the paper envelopes in which they were bought, or sometimes even without this protection. Records allowed to rub together in this way will quickly lose all beauty and vividness of tone. Unless you take better care of them, your records will never grow to be a varied library ; they will wear out too quickly. Moreover, every addition that you buy will but increase the muddle, causing more shuffling and friction of the precious discs every time you search for the piece you want to play.

Use a Filing System

The first necessity if you would preserve your records is a proper system of

Filing ; and if you would see your collection grow to goodly dimensions, and yet be able to place your hand on whichever disc you want, your filing must include a scientific method of CLASSIFICATION.

The system of filing adopted must, of course, be largely affected by the number of records to accommodate. For twelve records an ordinary album would be sufficient ; but generally the first suggestion to consider is whether one should purchase a record filing cabinet. One also has to decide the suitable size and type.

Fig. 2.—A RECORD FILING CABINET.

Holding 100 discs. Attached to the inside of the doors of the cabinet, which is a product of " His Master's Voice," is an index to the records.

Record Cabinets

There are many cabinets on the market, and they vary in capacity. One which is sponsored by " His Master's Voice " will hold 100 records. With the aid of a numbered list affixed inside the cabinet doors any record can be found instantly, and the record required is ejected automatically by lightly pressing a lever at the foot of each compartment.

Storage in the Gramophone Case

There are also pedestal gramophones with record compartments ; and special tables for " table grand " models generally have a shelf beneath on which record cases may be placed. One such table, which is quite a useful design, has a table surface 23 inches by 19 inches—just the right size for a table grand—and beneath

Fig. 3.—An "Atcraft" Record Cabinet.

Note the compartments to facilitate classification
of the records.

this is a cupboard divided into three
or four compartments in which 12-inch
and 10-inch records may be stored
upright.

Among other record filing cabinets
may be mentioned the "A. A. Brown,"
the "Jussrite" and the "Sesame." The
Globe-Wernicke Company, too, have
brought out an "Elastic" record cabinet
which is extensible on a similar principle
to the well-known bookcases.

Albums and Cases

Record albums and cases have also
much to recommend them, and these may
be stored either in a suitable cabinet or
on shelves. They should be kept upright,
like books, and should never on any
account be laid flat. Albums to hold
twelve records are supplied by the leading
gramophone firms, but these albums have
two disadvantages : they are heavy when
full, and the strain of carrying twelve
records tends to pull the album to pieces ;
at the same time their cost is rather high.
Cases are rather better, especially if one

likes to take records with one on
week-end holidays or when visiting
the house of a friend ; but cases, too,
are rather costly.

Two Six - Record Albums are Better than One Twelve-Record Album

If one's collection of records is at
all extensive it is best to obtain
cheaper albums made to hold six
records; it is possible to obtain albums
of this kind for from 10*d*. to 1*s*. 6*d*.
each. Then separate albums can be
devoted to records of music by each
important composer — an album for
Bach, Handel, Beethoven, and so on
—and the albums can be placed on
the shelves in chronological order,
the earliest composer first. The name
of the composer should be written on
the back of the album, and one or
two books should also be labelled
for Miscellaneous Orchestral, Instru-
mental, Operatic and Vocal Works.
In this way one's collection will be
carefully preserved, and the system
of classification will enable you, or

Fig. 4.—A Gramophone Table with Shelf
Beneath for Record Albums (H.M.V.).

Fig. 5.—How to Flatten Warped Records.

Place the records, after warming them in front of a fire, between sheets of plate-glass and leave them under a convenient weight for a length of time.

anyone else, to find any record that may be wanted.

Another System

Instead of using albums the records could be packed each in a stout manilla envelope. The envelopes could be numbered from one upwards at the top corner. It would also be necessary to keep a numbered, typewritten list, or a small notebook showing the place number of every record on the shelves.

An advantage of this system is that a greater number of records can be stored in a small space than is possible with albums ; but it also means that the shelves will have to bear a correspondingly greater weight. The shelves should therefore be somewhat shorter.

Record Shelves should be Strongly Constructed

These could be fitted in the recess beside a chimneybreast. They could be constructed of American whitewood or deal and could be stained any colour to suit the interior. The thickness of the wood should be not less than $\frac{3}{4}$ inch ; the depth of the shelves should be 13 inches for 12-inch records and 11 inches for 10-inch ones. The distance between each shelf should be not less than 13 inches.

It is not advisable for a shelf which supports records in albums to be more than 3 feet long. If the records are in envelopes the maximum length should be 2 feet. If the shelves exceed these measurements, they should be divided by solid partitions into spaces about 18 inches wide. There should also be a bracket support beneath the shelves in the centre ; and if the backs are boarded to exclude dust this also will increase the rigidity of the fitment.

The reason for these precautions is the enormous weight of the records. If the shelves sag, or if the records are loosely packed, they will tend to be thrown against one another instead of standing perpendicular. As a result, the records will be likely to warp. But if tightly and perpendicularly packed any tendency to warping will be corrected. In this respect albums which hold six records are better than envelopes. The covers of the albums act as supports and facilitate perpendicular storage.

So with Albums

On the other hand albums which hold twelve records are dangerous in that *if* the covers should bend they are strong and stout enough to pull the records with them, thereby causing them to warp instead of protecting them. Again, albums that hold six discs are superior.

Hints on Storing Records

To sum up, the following are the most important points to bear in mind :

1. Never store records flat, so that those beneath bear the weight of those above.

2. Never pack records loosely on shelves, so that by leaning at an angle of, say, 70 degrees, all the weight is thrown upon a dozen records or so at one end of the shelf. Stack them tightly, so that they will stand erect.

3. Divide the shelves into compartments 18 inches wide unless albums or cases are used.

Hints on Using Records

There are, of course, many other precautions which will help to prolong the life of records almost indefinitely. The following are some useful hints :—

1. Always dust each record with a soft cloth or record-dusting pad before playing. If dust is left on the disc it will be ground against the wax by the needle and the record will be affected.

2. Steel needles should be changed after each and every record. This hint should be almost unnecessary. The point of the needle, inevitably, is worn by playing, and this creates a cutting edge which, if the needle is used a second time, will plough through the delicate wax walls of the record grooves.

3. The motor should be wound while the turn-table is in motion. To start a record, gently move the needle into the record groove. Do not stab the needle down heavily on to the disc. Careless treatment of this kind will cause the record to start off with the opening bars terribly flat.

4. Never attempt to clean or improve records with oil. Sometimes an old record may be given a new lease of life by employing a specially fine needle, such as the Edison-Bell " Sympathetic Chromic."

5. If a record becomes badly scratched or cracked discard it. The crack may injure the delicate mechanism of the soundbox.

6. Modern electrical records are likely to be injured by playing them on an out-of-date gramophone. Electrical records require a specially responsive tone-arm. The weight borne by the needle should be approximately $3\frac{1}{2}$ ozs.

Does the Soundbox Swing from Side to Side ?

There is a more serious fault called " swinging " which is less frequently encountered. Swinging causes the soundbox to move from side to side, and is caused through the hole in the record not being in the exact centre of the record grooves. It may also result through the hole being too large for the spindle of the turn-table. Moreover, it is possible for a record to swing on one side of the disc and not on the other.

Curing the Fault

If the fault is only slight it may sometimes be cured by carefully enlarging the hole with a penknife, afterwards marking the label at the point which must be pressed against the spindle. If the swinging is more serious the centre hole should first be enlarged and then the record should be played over slowly, using a fibre needle to avoid the danger of scratching. Then tap the edge of the disc lightly until the record is centred on the turn-table as exactly as possible and the swinging is reduced to a minimum. Then you should take two small pieces of hard, but not too thick, cardboard, and cut a V in the edge of each. One side of the cardboard should then be coated with seccotine and should be applied to the record close up to the spindle. The second piece of cardboard should be applied to the other half of the hole, also touching the spindle. The record should then be left until the seccotine has set, when the result should be a record which is cured of swinging.

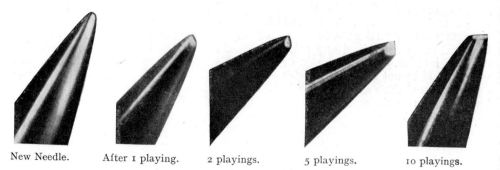

New Needle.   After 1 playing.   2 playings.   5 playings.   10 playings.

Fig. 6.—STEEL NEEDLE-POINT SHOWING WEAR AFTER PLAYING.
The needle-point is shown magnified to about 30 times its actual size.

Book-Tables With A Difference

ONE of the most popular pieces of furniture for the lounge or living-room is an eight-sided table-book-case standing a little under 2 feet high. These tables are generally constructed of either oak or walnut, and bookshelves are fitted along the four wider sides of the table. Two interesting variations of this idea are seen in the illustrations. One example, in Fig. 1, depicts a work-table book-case, and another, in Fig. 2, a cock-tail bookcase. The former embodies, in addition to bookshelves round the sides, a dustproof internal compartment enclosed by a double sliding top in which needlework and materials are stored. A great advantage of this work-table book-case is that the needlework is quite invisible when put away, and there is nothing to indicate that the table has another use.

The cocktail bookcase has a neatly concealed compartment at either end, one of which is shown opened in Fig. 2. These compartments are for bottles, syphons and glasses.

The needlework bookcase would also be suitable for several other purposes. The compartment beneath the sliding top

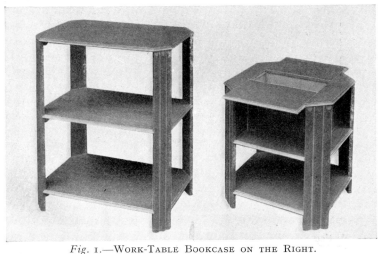

*Fig. 1.—*Work-Table Bookcase on the Right.

could be used as a medicine chest, a spirit and liqueur cabinet, for magazines and newspapers or correspondence files. If the book-table were employed in a man's bedroom it could be used for clean collars and handkerchiefs.

The cocktail bookcase is also suitable for other purposes— a smoker's table, for example. A strip of wood with some round holes for pipes is easily attached to the inner side of the flap.

*Fig. 2.—*Two More Book-Tables—A Cocktail Bookcase on the Left.

How
CHINA

BLOOR
1815–1839

BLOOR
1815–1831

Two examples of marks used by this Derbyshire works. The first, showing a crown and letter B, should not be confused with the Crown Derby mark.

Bow RARE

The first example is a rare mark used by the early Bow potters, from a specimen form in the Hitchin Manor House Collection. The figures and statuettes produced at the Stratf le-Bow works were seldom marked. Usual marks are the arrow, bow and arrow, and anch The anchor and sword combined is usually found in brown or red on the folds of statue

Bow
1730–1775

Bow
1730–1775

Bow
1730–1775

BRISTOL
1770
An early mark probably used by William Cookworthy.

CAUGHLEY
1757–1834
Crescent in outline, usually in blue under-glaze.

CAUGHLEY
1757–1834
The initial letter S in blue refers to Shropshire or Salopian ware, often attributed to T. Turner.

CAUGHLEY
1757–1834
Shaded crescent. Another example of the Caughley mark.

CAUGHLEY
1757–1834
Two examples of numerals, in the Chinese style, associated with the influence of Chinese pottery on British designers.

CAUGHLEY
1757–1834

CHAMPION BR
1773–178
Mark used on porcelain duri time the work under the con Richard Cham

---

CHELSEA–DERBY
About 1773
The Derby crown and Chelsea anchor marks combined, indicative of the combination of these two works.

DERBY
About 1769
Initial mark, usually in red.

CROWN DERBY
1773–1782

CROWN DERBY
circa 1780

The Derby marks usually incorporate a crown and the letter D, the crowns becoming more elabor drawn as time passes. The initial letter in early specimens is separated by batons, while in examples the initial is surrounded by scroll work, ultimately becoming incorporated in the ornam scroll work.

DERBY
1773–1782

DERBY
1780–1782

DER

MINTON
1790
An imitation of the Sevres mark, it is one of the earliest Minton marks.

MINTON
1851
A bold design for a distinctive mark.

NANTGARW
1813–1820
The products of this Welsh works are distinguished by the name, incised or coloured.

PLYMOUTH
1768–1772

PLYMOUTH
1768–1772

PLYMOUTH
1768–1772

PLYM
1768–

The Plymouth works, in common with those at Bristol, are notable an English factories as the only places where true porcelain analogous Chinese was produced. The usual mark is the alchemical symbol for t Arabic numerals 2 and 4 conjoined. Rarely used variants are also show

---

Chamberlain Worcester

CHAMBERLAIN–WORCESTER.
1784–1840
Another example of literal marks, in this the maker's name and the place of origin.

WORCESTER
1751

WORCESTER
1751

WORCESTER
1751

WORCESTER
178

Worcester was the third of the great English factories, and was destined to become the important. The products are distinguished by various marks, several examples of which reproduced. The solid blue crescent is a rare and early mark, as is the crescent with prof

Know
MARKS

 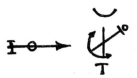

Bow	Bow	Bow	Bow	BRISTOL	BRISTOL	BRISTOL

Bow 1730–1775 · further examples of the anchor ks used at the Bow works. They akin to the Chelsea marks, but are inguishable by the nature of the celain on which they appear.

Bow 1730–1775

Bow 1730–1775 In these specimens the arrow is treated as a weather vane with the letter E; the anchor is crossed and a simple bow-shaped symbol placed above it.

Bow 1730–1775

BRISTOL 1768–1770 A plain cross, as here shown, is the customary mark on Bristol porcelain.

BRISTOL 1768–1770 This mark, in gold, was followed by a numeral indicative of the individual potter. The numbers range from 1 to 24.

BRISTOL About 1776 Crossed swords, akin to the Meissen mark, is found on a number of pieces made at the Bristol works.

CHELSEA 1748–1770 chor on an ised back- ound, sur- nded by an l.

CHELSEA 1748–1770 The triangle sign was usually incised and was often dated.

CHELSEA 1745 A variation of the triangle, with name and date. An early and rare specimen.

CHELSEA 1750–1770 The anchor is the most distinctive Chelsea mark, often embossed in gold or colour.

CHELSEA 1750–1770 Two variations of the anchor design, sometimes dated, usually in red or brown, and found in the drapery of figures or on the stand.

CHELSEA 1750–1770

CHELSEA–DERBY circa 1774 The combined mark of the Chelsea and Derby factories, adopted when the Chelsea works were sold to Duesbury. Usually in red or gold.

DERBY 1751–1769 variation of early initial er, with the rd Derby in pt.

DERBY MODERN The initial letter D is here shown cleverly duplicated and in the form of a scroll.

CROWN DERBY 1780–1815 Another variant of the crown, batons and initial mark used at the Derby works.

DUESBURY & KEAN 1795 A distinctive mark used at a time when Duesbury was in partnership with Kean.

DERBY RARE The crossed swords of Dresden, in early and rare use at Derby.

LONGTON HALL 1757–1758 Initial letters of Longton and Littler, similar to the W mark used by Wegali of Berlin. Principally used on table ware.

LONGPORT 1773–1835 A place name used as a distinguishing mark on the products of the Longport works.

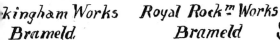

ROCKINGHAM circa 1840

ROCKINGHAM circa 1850

SALOPIAN or **CAUGHLEY** 1757–1834

SWANSEA circa 1810 The characteristic symbol of this Welsh product is the trident, usually impressed, and sometimes with the word Swansea in script.

SWANSEA circa 1810

eral marks or place-names, to identify the manufacturer of chinaware, are in very extensive , including such famous names as Spode, Copeland, Wedgwood, Doulton, and others. Three mples are given. The first two show interesting variations, the third, impressed in the china paste, ongs to the Caughley works and is an exception to the rule.

WORCESTER About 1770

WORCESTER Early Blue

WORCESTER About 1760

WORCESTER About 1763

WORCESTER About 1763

WORCESTER About 1765

WORCESTER About 1765

se further examples of Worcester china marks show, from left ight, a mark in the Chinese style; an early mark usually in blue; ariant of the blue W but with a feathered tail. The significance he next two marks showing crossed swords is unknown, but it is frequently found in underglaze blue on early pieces, details of the swords vary, and the numbers are either 9 or 91. The last two specimens are in the Chinese style, in underglaze blue, usually on early pieces decorated in blue in the manner of Old Nankin china.

NEEDLEWORK STITCHES

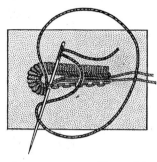

Fig. 1.—BUTTONHOLES IN DRESS MATERIALS.

If the material is liable to fray, the edges of the slit should be wetted with gum and allowed to dry before working. Two threads of coarse silk or fine cord should be laid along the edge and worked in. Draw them in when finished.

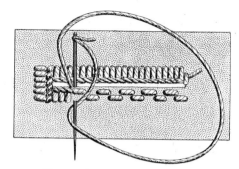

Fig. 2.—BUTTONHOLES IN LINEN.

Mark out the length by means of two rows of running stitches in opposite directions and make the slit between them. For buttonholes in linen use thread. Work from left to right, as shown in the picture above.

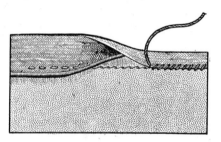

Fig. 3.—BINDING WITH BRAID OR GALON.

Use the back-stitch and ease the braid during stitching, to allow for shrinkage in the wash, otherwise it may pucker the material.

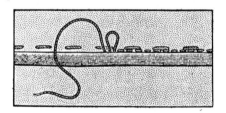

Fig. 4.—STITCHING ON PIPING.

Tack the cord lightly on, and back-stitch the piping to the material with small stitches. Fold in the row outside edges and fell like an ordinary hem.

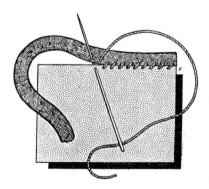

Fig. 5.—SEWING ON ROUND CORD.

Use a strong thread and hem with small, close stitches, and to avoid twisting keep the plait formed by the threads of the cord always in a straight line.

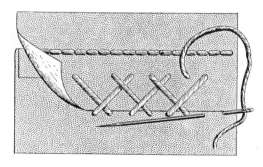

Fig. 6.—HERRING-BONING.

This stitch is used for seams in flannel and for over-casting dress seams. It is done from left to right. It is also a useful stitch for decorative needlework.

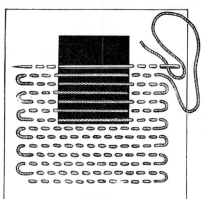

Fig. 7.

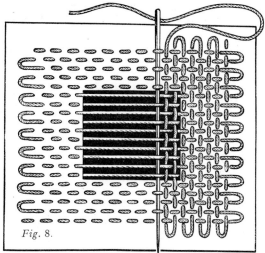

Fig. 8.

Figs. 7, 8 and 9.—LINEN DARNING.

Fig. 7.—All darns should be worked on the wrong side of the material. The longitudinal running to form the warp should be done first, as shown in Fig. 7. The thread must not be drawn tight as the new thread will shrink in the wash. Always cover more ground than is actually required to cover the hole.

Fig. 8.—The woof threads would be worked in and out of the warp threads, as shown in Fig. 8. Care should be taken to leave loops at the ends and to keep an even tension on the threads. It is sometimes an advantage to use a double thread for the woof, especially in cases where the material is subject to hard wear.

Fig. 9.—In some materials it is an advantage to form a diagonal web across the warp threads, as shown in Fig. 9.

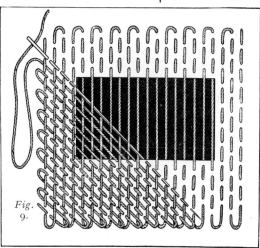

Fig. 9.

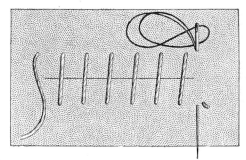

Fig. 10.—PREPARING RENT FOR FINE DRAWING.

The needle is threaded with fine silk or hair, which is woven backwards and forwards into the thickness of the cloth.

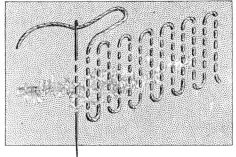

Fig. 11.—INVISIBLE DARNING.

The rent is drawn together and the broken threads are then worked in. Broken edge may be drawn together by a thread matching the material or by a ravelling.

STAINING AND POLISHING FLOORS

THERE are several things to be taken into consideration when selecting a suitable stain and polish for the floor—the kind of wood from which it is made, the condition of the surface, suitability of colour, and the question of expense. But the most important is the condition of the floor, for even the best of stains and polishes can only be applied successfully if the conditions are suitable. Most of the failures to obtain a really good stained and polished surface are due to lack of preparation rather than the unsuitability of the material used.

There are so many preparations on the market that a selection of a suitable stain, and an accompanying polish, is somewhat bewildering. To go to a shop and buy a floor polish is not enough ; it is necessary to know just the most suitable form of finish that the particular kind of floor requires. New boards with a pleasing grain and a good colour should be treated quite differently from those made from cheap wood. Flooring of hardwood will probably look much more effective with a polish only, while a softwood floor must be treated with a suitable preparation to prevent undue absorption of the covering liquid.

NEW FLOORS
Examine the Boards for Nails and Roughness

As most of the modern houses are floored with deal boards and are not so carefully nailed as they might be, the first thing to do is to see that there are no projecting nails and no unplaned surfaces. It is important that the wood should be quite smooth.

Then Wash the Surface

The next thing to do is to wash the boards with a stiff brush and warm water. Soap and soap powder should be avoided, but if the floor is very dirty and a solvent, such as soap is necessary, all traces should be rinsed off afterwards with clean water. Soda in any form should be avoided. When the floor is dry, clean paper should be spread about so that no marks are made on the clean surface.

Treating Soft Wood Before Staining

Deal and similar soft woods have an open grain and unless the pores are filled up they will soak up a considerable amount of stain and polish. As well, some portions of the grain will absorb more than others, thus causing a patchy and unsatisfactory finish. Another form of trouble likely to be experienced in staining soft wood is the liability of the grain to rise in ridges along the softer portions. This is particularly noticeable in yellow deal, a wood often used for flooring.

Making Filler for Soft Wood

A satisfactory and easily prepared filler can be made from powdered whiting made into a paste by adding size. Whiting

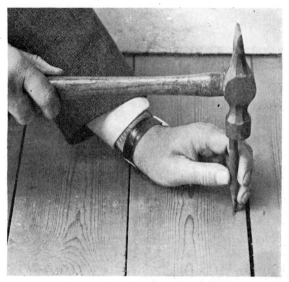

Fig. 1.—THE FIRST THING TO DO.
Projecting nails should be driven just below the surface with a nail punch before any other work is attempted.

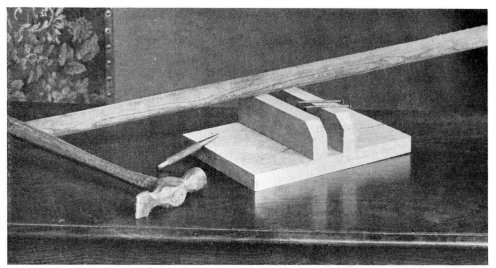

Fig. 2 —Parts of an Easily-Made Appliance for use in Floor Polishing.

is obtainable in lumps quite inexpensively and will powder easily with a little pressure, but unless it is quite dry, it should be placed in a warm oven before use. It is an advantage to rub the powder through a fine sieve, but with a little patience a sufficiently fine granulation can be obtained by using an ordinary vegetable presser in a shallow bowl, such as a washhand basin. The size can be obtained in jelly form and melted in a pot over a very low gas flame, or the

Fig. 3.—The Appliance in Use.

Smoothing the floor surface with pumice powder after applying a filler to the floor. Instead of pumice powder, the floor can be rubbed with glasspaper. This should be attached to the underside of the appliance.

material can be purchased in powder form as concentrated size and dissolved in hot water. The powdered whiting should be added very gradually to the melted size, stirring well until a creamy paste results.

Applying the Filler

Paste fillers are generally applied to the surface with a stiff brush, a worn large varnish or similar brush is useful, but a cheap nail brush answers quite well. The paste is first brushed across the grain, and then in its direction, care being taken to use enough. An excess of paste is troublesome to remove when dry owing to the dust raised in the process. It is an advantage to have at hand a pad formed by several thicknesses of soft rag, which may be damped with a thinned solution of size. A brisk rub with the pad will soon remove the surplus filler and leave an even surface.

Another Useful Filler to Use

Another filler can be made with superfine plaster of paris in the same way, but it requires a little more care in mixing. It is useful when a hard surface is required.

Smoothing

In all cases it is necessary to leave the surface quite smooth after a filler has been used. One method of treatment is to rub the wood with No. 1 glasspaper. In the case of a large surface it is convenient to make an appliance so that the rubbing may be done more expediously. Cut a piece of 1-inch thick board, 11 by 6 inches, and screw on two 2 by 1 by 6-inch strips, 1 inch apart, as indi-

cated in Fig. 2. Insert between the strips, at a convenient angle, a broomstick, and then nail or screw it to the strips, placing an angle piece at the back. The face of the block of wood should be covered with a piece of thick felt stuck firmly in position with glue or seccotine. A felt cover can be secured with drawing-pins, as shown in Fig. 3, and if a little pumice powder is sprinkled over the floor and the felt rubber applied to the surface in the direction of the grain, a smooth surface is rapidly obtained. It is important, with this method of treating

Fig. 4.—FILLING UP SPACES WITH PLASTIC WOOD.

the surface, to remove all traces of the pumice powder with a soft brush before staining.

Filling Cracks and Holes in the Wood

Although a paste filler applied with a brush will be effective enough in filling the pores of the wood, the cracks and holes may require the use of a knife to fill them properly and firmly. Large cracks and holes, especially where they are likely to experience wear, should be filled with " Necol " plastic wood, as shown in Fig. 4. This preparation is simple to use and when hard can be rubbed down perfectly smooth with glasspaper. Plastic wood is

*Fig. 5.—*APPLYING STAIN WITH A SPONGE.

Work along two or three boards at a time to avoid overlapping, and see that the finishing strokes
are in the direction of the grain.

also useful in many other ways and it is economical to invest in a large tin. Putty is often suggested as a suitable material for filling cracks and holes, but not when the wood is to be stained.

Is the Filling Suitable?

The above preliminaries are essential if a thoroughly satisfactory job is to be made of water staining and varnishing. Although filling the wood and subsequent smoothing with pumice powder takes time and a considerable amount of energy, the quality of the resulting work makes it well worth while. It should be noted that the success of a stain depends on the manner in which the liquid penetrates into the grain. It is, therefore, necessary that the filling should be absorbent. It is often an advantage to tint the filling to the colour of the stain, but with ordinary care it is not necessary. In purchasing ready prepared filling, care should be taken that it is suitable for use with water stain.

Making Inexpensive Water Stains

Water stains may be obtained in liquid form ready for immediate use. They are quite inexpensive, but the cheapest method of providing the stain is to use powder, and mix with water to the required strength. A large number of colours are available, and it is possible to consider the general colour scheme of the room in the matter of staining as in that of the painting and the wallpaper. For example, there is a wide range of colour in aniline dyes that are soluble in water, in addition there are many vegetable dyes that are just as suitable for wood as for fabric. There are also inexpensive spirit stains, such as "Ancolac," that are particularly effected.

What Colour Shall I Use?

Although it is usual to stain floors to imitate the colouring of oak, mahogany and walnut, for example, there is no reason why such colours as green, blue, purple should not be used. It is, of course, necessary to use a clear varnish, or in the case of wax polish, to stain the

Fig. 6.—Varnishing should be done with a Wide Brush.
Note the unfilled space between the boards.

wax used in the first applications of the finish. The dry colours used should be of superfine quality. Brunswick and vandyke browns, burnt sienna and venetian red are generally used for floor stains.

A Black Water Stain

For a black water stain, place 1 lb. of logwood chips in 2 quarts of water and bring it up to boiling-point and simmer for one hour. Also dissolve 1 ounce of green copperas in 1 quart of hot water, and use it as a following coat to the logwood solution.

When the particular stain has been chosen, bring it up to boiling-point and add one part of vinegar to eight parts of stain.

Applying the Stain

The actual staining should be carried out as rapidly as possible and in the direction of the grain. Either a wide brush or a sponge can be used, the latter is generally preferable as the work can be carried out with greater rapidity. It is advisable, when using a sponge, to wear rubber gloves, or to wipe some vaseline over the hands. Do not apply too much stain at one time, and in no case leave pools of the liquid on the wood. Care should be taken to avoid overlapping, and it will be found advisable to take two or three boards at a time, working down the whole length. If the depth of colour is not enough, it is better to obtain the required shade by a second coat rather than attempt to obtain it with one application. In some cases it will be necessary to work in the stain from side to side, but the finishing strokes must always be in the direction of the grain, as shown in Fig. 5.

A Quicker Alternative Treatment

As an alternative treatment, when it is inconvenient to take the time for the preliminary filling, the staining can be done first after the floor has been thoroughly cleaned. The above method of applying the stain should be followed, and it should be noted that the wood will absorb a considerable quantity. The filler can be strong size applied hot and rubbed down with pumice powder when quite dry. A better but more expensive filler is shellac varnish thinned down with spirit. This should also be rubbed down with pumice when hard.

Finishing the Stained Floor — Varnishing

There are two commonly used methods of finishing a stained floor—varnishing and waxing. The best way of using varnish is to obtain best quality hard floor varnish, or that used for church seats.

A first coat should be applied with the varnish diluted with pure turpentine, not more than one part of turpentine to four parts of varnish, and should be allowed to dry thoroughly, leaving it as long as possible. In all cases allow the varnish to flow easily from a wide brush working in the direction of the grain, as indicated in Fig. 6. At least two days should be allowed between the applications and special care should be taken in the meantime to keep the surface free from dust.

Rapid Methods of Varnishing — Varnish Stains

Time can be saved by giving the surface a first coat of good shellac varnish, but it should be rubbed down with glasspaper or pumice powder if a good surface is required. The prepared varnish stains provide a very rapid method of staining a floor, but it should be understood that it is the varnish that is coloured and very little of the stain contained in it penetrates into the grain of the wood. These varnish stains are very liable to show scratches, and to peel off the wood. When this trouble does happen, it is a very trying job to remove the old coating in order to renew it.

Satisfactory Prepared Stains

The only really satisfactory form of prepared stain is that with an oil base, known as oil varnish stain. Completely satisfactory work can be carried out with the preparation known as " Fastain." It is made to imitate oak, satinwood, walnut, mahogany, rosewood and ebony. If, when quite dry, a matter of about 6 hours, it is given a coat of hard church

varnish, a thoroughly durable finish is produced. It has exceptionally good covering properties; 1 pint will cover 120 square feet, and, being transparent, it helps to enhance the natural beauty of the grain.

Floors to be Waxed do not Need Filling

Floors that are to be waxed should be stained with water stain as suggested above and need not be filled.

Rapid Staining

Rapid methods of staining can be done with dry powder colours ground in turps and diluted to a suitable consistency and strength. Wood dyes such as " Colron," for example, are particularly effective, as they penetrate and do not hide the grain of the wood.

Waxing

The actual waxing can be done with ordinary beeswax dissolved in pure turpentine to a creamy consistency. The wax should be applied in the first place with a stiff brush and then polished with a rubber. The simply-made appliance, illustrated in Fig. 2, can be used for the purpose, if covered with two or three thicknesses of suitable cloth as in Fig. 7. Floor polish can be applied direct to the stain in the same way and forms an excellent and inexpensive substitute for the pure wax and turpentine.

Oil Stains—How to Apply Them

Oil stains are equally effective on softwood as well as hardwood floors. The stain is applied with a wide brush directly to the wood before it is filled, working in the direction of the grain. The best results are obtained when the wood is perfectly smooth and it is, therefore, advisable to give the floor a preliminary rub with glasspaper. When the stain is quite dry the surface can be waxed or varnished. Before varnishing it is advisable to rub the whole of the surface over with a soft cloth moistened with methylated spirit. This treatment provides a bite for the varnish and allows it to take much easier.

Finishing Hardwood Floors

Parquetry, wood block and other hardwood floors can be finished with clear varnish and given a high polish by first applying a coat of clear shellac varnish thinned down with methylated spirit. This coating should be rubbed down with glasspaper or pumice powder, and when all the dust has been removed from the surface, a well distributed coating of best hard copal varnish should be applied.

Apply Varnish Thinly

It is a mistake to cover floors thickly with varnish ; it is sure to chip off with

stained floors in bad condition require special treatment. The particular treatment depends on the manner in which the floor has been done before. Reconditioning varnished floors, for example, that have not been stained is a simple matter compared with those that have, especially those treated with thick varnish stains.

First—Clean the Whole Surface

In all cases before anything is done, the whole of the surface should be thoroughly cleansed with soap and water, rinsed effectively, and then allowed to dry free from dust.

Fig. 7.—The Appliance Used as a Floor Polisher.

wear. The thin coating is also more suitable for the subsequent application of wax floor polish. When once a floor has been properly treated with varnish and is kept polished regularly with a good preparation, it will be thoroughly durable. It is as well to point out that on no account should a floor be polished with wax polish until all the dust has been removed from the surface. If this is neglected the surface will become gritty and lose its brilliance.

Re-Polishing and Re-Staining Floors

All the above instructions apply to the treatment of new floors ; polished and

Renewing Worn Varnished Surface

To renew the surface of a varnished floor, the remaining gloss should be removed with glasspaper or pumice powder. If, however, it is a stained as well as a varnished floor, and the stain has worn in places, the cleaning must be carried farther. In the first case a fresh coat of varnish will generally suffice, and the surface can be treated with " Fastain." Instead of re-varnishing, the floor can be finished with a wax polish or with plain beeswax and turpentine well rubbed in. Owing to the previous filling, only a thin coating of varnish or wax will be needed.

Treating to Remove Varnish

Floors in bad condition should have the entire coating of varnish removed with strong soda solution, but this will answer only with thin surfaces. Heavily varnished floors should be treated with a varnish remover. There are several preparations available, that known as "Stripso" is particularly effective for the purpose. The remover is applied to the surface, generally with a brush, and when the varnish softens it can be peeled off with a knife or scraper. The surface is now washed over with a rag soaked in benzine or turpentine to remove all traces of the preparation.

To Remove Stain

If the floor, after the treatment with the varnish remover, is still stained in patches, it will be necessary to apply a bleaching solution. One of the most effective methods of dealing with the discoloured surface is to use a strong solution of oxalic acid crystals, but the greatest care must be used, as it is poisonous. The solution should be brushed over the surface and left in pools in places where the stain is deepest. Do not remove the solution until the stains have disappeared entirely, then the surplus can be wiped off and the surface cleaned with hot water, rinsing it several times.

Rub Down Surfaces

Surfaces that have been cleaned with varnish remover, whether subsequently bleached or not, should be rubbed down when dry with glasspaper or pumice powder.

Treat with Oil Stain

The powder should be entirely cleaned off and then the surface should be treated with a penetrating oil stain. Water stains are entirely unsuitable and should on no account be used. The special preparations sold for varnishing floors are not all suitable for renovations. "Fastain" may be used, as also "Colron" wood dye.

Filling after Staining May be Necessary

Surfaces that have not been bleached need not be filled as a rule, but with particularly porous wood it is an advantage to give the surface, after staining, a coat of shellac varnish. It should be noted that shellac should not be applied on an undersurface of varnish, only as a preparation for varnishing to provide a better gloss, or as a finish in itself.

Filling in Cracks between Boards— Another Method.

Cracks between the boards can be filled in with beeswax. To enable this to be done the wax must be softened by heating gently, which is conveniently done by putting the wax into an earthenware jar, placing it into a saucepan, raising the water to boiling point, and keeping it simmering until the wax has dissolved.

While in use, the jar of wax should be placed in a basin of boiling water, which must be warmed up from time to time as necessary. The wax can be worked into cracks with a piece of stick and a hot metal trowel, but this back-aching work may be obviated by tying several thicknesses of coarse linen around the shoes and working the wax into place with a shuffling movement of the feet.

Preparing a Floor for Dancing.

If a dance is to be held in a room having a plain board floor it is most desirable that it have some preparation, although it may only be used on one or a few occasions.

First of all, examine the whole floor and pull out or hammer down any nails that may be projecting, and remove any roughness by rubbing with coarse sandpaper.

Unless the floor can be waxed—which is rather a lengthy process—it will be desirable to treat the surface with powdered chalk. This should be spread evenly over the floor and then well worked into the cracks and pores of the wood by means of an old broom, which should be wrapped in a thick piece of sacking or other coarse, fluffless material.

This acts as a rubber and does not throw up so much dust as if the broom were used in the usual way. All surplus chalk should be worked to one part of the floor and then removed with dustpan and brush.

An Embroidered Afternoon Tea Cloth

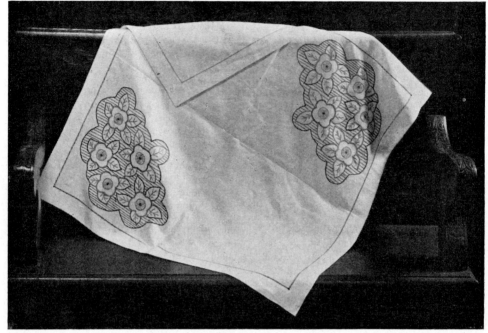

Fig. 1.—Embroidery Made Easy.

By following the simple instructions given in the following article, and using the design transfer, no difficulty will be found in making the above attractive embroidered afternoon tea cloth in white linen, with a hemstitched border.

EMBROIDERY is one of the most delightful means of expressing colour, charm, and individuality in the home, as well as for personal decoration.

To embroider is to apply certain patterns to various types of material with silks, cottons, or flax threads. The forms must be expressed by the worker in the arranging of varied stitches for fillings of flower and leaf forms.

Learning How to Embroider

The first thing would be to learn as many of the stitches as possible; secondly, to study the growth, form, and colour of flowers, plants, birds, and butterflies.

Many colour schemes can be derived from the beauties of nature, but the worker must be careful to avoid imitating the natural appearances of flowers and leaves, so that the finished piece of work does not resemble a painting.

What to Embroider

There are many things in the home that can be made so much more interesting if embroidered. A table can be beautified by means of a table runner or centre worked in gaily coloured cottons or silks on linen or British satin.

A daintily-worked tea cosy or afternoon tea cloth, which must be of washable materials, will add charm to the tea-table. Gaily coloured cushions, screens, hangings, chair backs, all go to make the rooms more cheerful and attractive.

An Afternoon Tea Cloth

An afternoon tea cloth of white linen with a hemstitched border is illustrated in Fig. 1. The design is a bold conventional type of groups of flowers and simple leaves (*see* Fig. 2). It is worked in opposite corners of the cloth in Clark's Stranded Cottons.

These cottons are very reliable. There is a large range of colours, and they are inexpensive and will wash beautifully. The colours chosen for this particular piece of work are three shades of blue and two of yellow.

Fig. 2.—THE DESIGN.

The lettering shown above is referred to in the text in order to indicate where to employ the different embroidery stitches and what colour of thread to use.

The colour scheme can be changed in many ways to suit the taste of the worker, according to the room or tea service.

Materials Required

White Old Bleach Linen, No. E.L. 45, 1 yard (36 inches wide). No. 7 embroidery needles, 1 packet. Clark's Stranded Cottons : 3 skeins of Dark Blue, No. 510 F ; 2 skeins of Mid-Blue, No. 508 F ;

2 skeins of Light Blue, No. 507 F ; 1 skein of Light Yellow, No. 514 F ; 2 skeins of Darker Yellow, No. 515 F. One reel of Coat's white cotton, No. 50, for hemstitching.

Preparing the Cloth

The corners of the cloth are mitred. To do this correctly, accurate folding and measuring are necessary. Crease very firmly, keeping to the thread of the linen, the first turn about $\frac{1}{4}$ inch wide (AA), Fig. 3 ; then the width of hem, $1\frac{1}{2}$ inch (BB).

Open out, thus showing two creases in each direction, as indicated in the diagram. Now turn down the corner diagonally at C, taking care that one crease B falls on the other, bringing the outer corner over to position D. The corner is then cut away about $\frac{1}{4}$ inch from the turning on the dotted line DD, giving the result indicated by Fig. 4.

Leave the fold over on the slope, and refold first on the outer creases, then the inner ones, so getting the final position shown in Fig. 5, where the dotted lines give the position of the edges of the linen that are tucked inside. The corner must now be slip-stitched together, starting at point A and working down to B.

Doing the Hemstitching

The cloth is then ready for hemstitching. Draw out 8 threads, cutting them in the corner at B, Fig. 5. The hem must be carefully tacked down to the top of line made by the pulling of threads.

Fig. 6 shows method of working. The needle is brought through at the left side of the threads, and then passed from right to left, taking up 3 or 4 threads. Pull

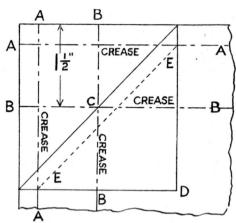

Fig. 3.—MAKING THE HEM—FIRST STAGE.
Where to crease the cloth preparatory to folding over the edges and mitreing the corners.

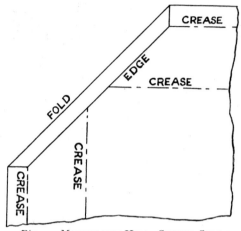

Fig. 4.—MAKING THE HEM—SECOND STAGE.
Cutting and folding cloth at corners to make the mitre.

through and place the needle in again, taking up a piece of the ground material and hem. Pull the thread tightly so that the bundles are quite defined. Hemstitching is worked from left to right. The same idea is carried out on the opposite side of the bundles of threads.

Transferring the Design to the Cloth

Having prepared the cloth, the next step is to transfer the design on to the linen. In this instance this is made easy by using the transfer on the chart which accompanies this article. Full instructions for using the transfer are given on page 136.

When a transfer is not used, a full-size drawing must be made. This should be traced on to a sheet of strong tracing paper, leaving a good margin of plain paper. The method of pouncing shown on page 13 can be employed for transferring the design on to the linen.

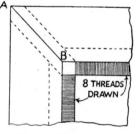

Fig. 5.—MAKING THE HEM—THIRD STAGE.
Draw out eight threads, cutting them in the corner at B. This also shows how the edges of the cloth are folded over and how the cloth is mitred at the corners.

Take a pricker, which can be made by fixing a needle into a piece of cork, and prick very small holes all round the outline of design. The finer the pricking of the holes the better line one can get. Very long lines in bold designs can be pricked with a tracing wheel. Always turn the tracing over before pricking, as best results are obtained with the pouncing when the rough side of the holes are uppermost. A felt stair pad is very handy to use when pricking the designs.

Having finished this stage, fix the tracing carefully on to the linen by means of drawing pins. A soft round pad can be made by means of rolling a strip of linen, as shown in Fig. 7, and sewing it. This is dipped in some finely powdered charcoal, procured from a chemist's shop, and lightly rubbed over the pricked lines in one direction, taking care not to rub too much on, as it is apt to soil the material. Then carefully remove the tracing, and there should be a clear, defined dotted line.

Colouring the Design

Now you must have a small tube of light red watercolour, a fine

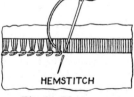

Fig. 6.—METHOD OF WORKING THE HEMSTITCH.

brush (No. 4), a palette, and a small jar of water handy. Squeeze a little colour on to the palette and mix with water, do not have it too thin, as it is apt to run when painting, making a heavy untidy line. A design that is clearly painted on is so much easier to work. When the painting is finished allow it to dry, finally dusting off any traces of charcoal. Now all is ready for working.

Fig. 7.—For Transferring the Design.

Soft pad made of a roll of linen for rubbing powdered charcoal through a dotted transfer.

Ready for Embroidering

It is essential to have a thimble, a pair of small sharply-pointed scissors, and suitable crewel needles. So many workers use needles that are too large and thick, thus making it so much harder to work. It is better to work the background first, shown by broken lines in the pattern. The stitch used is a laid oriental stitch.

Working the Laid Oriental Stitch

To proceed, take a piece of dark blue stranded cotton which is made up of 6 threads, use two of these threads. Fasten neatly at the back and bring out to the front at A, Fig. 8. The cotton is then taken to the back at B, and brought out again at C, ready for the next line. Thread a needle with the dark yellow, and bring out on the left side of the line at D. Couch with a slanting stitch at intervals, always working in a downward direction. This can be managed by turning the cloth

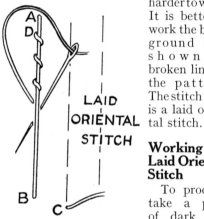

Fig. 8.—Method of Working the Laid Oriental Stitch.

This stitch is used for the background.

round when the line commencing at C is begun.

The design is made up of five groups, each consisting of a flower surrounded by leaves. The stitches used in the working of these flowers and leaves are Stem, Chain, and Buttonhole.

Stem or Outline Stitch

The stem or outline stitch is the simplest of all. To work, take 2 threads of stranded cotton, fasten on the back neatly, bring to the front and commence with a half-stitch. Then keeping the thread downwards and to the right, place your needle in so as to bring it out about 3 threads above the half-stitch. For the next stitch the needle is put $\frac{1}{8}$ inch above the last stitch, and brought out again about 3 threads higher (see Fig. 9).

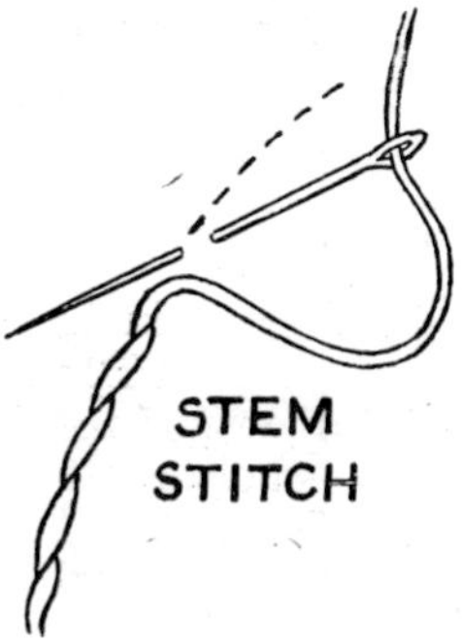

Chain-Stitch

Fasten on at the back and bring through to the front (see Fig. 10). Keep the thread in position with the left thumb. Place the needle in the hole through which the thread was brought out. Take about $\frac{1}{8}$ inch of material on the needle and pull the thread through; this makes the first link of the chain-stitch. The longer the stitch required the more material should be taken up on the needle. Care should be taken not to pull the thread too tight, as it is apt to pucker the material, especially when working on the cross.

Fig. 10.—Method of Working the Chain-Stitch.

Stem or Outline Stitch

STEM STITCH

Fig. 9.—Working the Stem-Stitch.

Employed for embroidering the flowers and outlining the whole design.

Buttonhole or Blanket Stitch

Place the needle in at A, taking up a piece of material AB (Fig. 11), keeping the thread under the needle, and to the right each time.

This stitch can be varied in many ways, by altering the length of stitch in groups, as shown in Fig. 11, C and D, working, for instance, two short and two long buttonhole stitches close together. Fig. 11, D, shows two rows of single buttonhole stitches worked one row into the other in two colours.

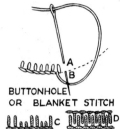

BUTTONHOLE OR BLANKET STITCH

Fig. 11.—BUTTONHOLE OR BLANKET STITCH.

Summary of Stitches and Colours

Each of the five groups of the design shown in Fig. 2 are lettered A, B, C, D, E. The following table gives the worker a general idea of the stitches combined.

A.—Leaves are worked in Middle Blue in Chain.
Veins are worked in Stem in Dark Yellow.
Flowers are worked in Light Blue in Buttonhole.
Centres are worked in two shades of Yellow in long and short Buttonhole.

B.—Leaves in Light Blue in Chain.
Veins in Dark Yellow in Stem.
Flowers in Middle Blue in Buttonhole.
Centres in two shades of Yellow in long and short Buttonhole, as in A.

C.—Leaves in Dark Blue in Stem.
Flowers in Light Blue in Buttonhole.
Veins and Centres as before.

D.—Same as A.

E.—Same as C.

The small centres of each flower are worked in close buttonhole in dark blue, the heading of the stitch is on the outside of the small circle.

The whole design outlined in stem-stitch.

HOW TO USE A TRANSFER

A transfer is a very ready means for getting a pattern marked on a piece of material. The embroiderers' method, already described, of first making a full-sized tracing, then pricking, pouncing and painting is all avoided. The transfer which will be found with this article is, therefore, of great service, as the process of ironing on can be done quickly and easily. A little care is necessary, the material must be dry, and the iron moderately hot.

Arranging Transfer on Material

Stretch the linen quite flat on an ironing blanket or board, and pin the transfer in place face down. Be sure to fix it in the exact position required and, with a pattern that has to be straight, with the edge of the material. Make sure that the border space left is parallel, and of the same width. Nothing looks more unsightly in finished work than a crooked appearance of the applied design.

Using the Iron

A transfer can only be used once. Apply the iron directly to the paper, using a slight pressure, and making sure every part of the surface is pressed. Do not be too vigorous in moving the iron about, or the transfer may get rucked up. Usually, a transfer has the title and publisher's name, and instructions on the edge, the pattern and the wording of transfer being printed in the same ink. Therefore, if the iron is allowed to touch these parts, the words will be found on the material. This must be avoided, as the ink is fairly fast and not easily removed. It is best to cut the printing off the transfer before using it.

Cover Transfer Lines with the Stitches

Also for the same reason, when working a pattern placed on by means of a transfer, always let the stitches just cover the line and so avoid any need for washing. Usually two or three washings are necessary before the line is completely removed.

COMMON COMPLAINTS AND THEIR TREATMENT

IN dealing with the treatment of common complaints in the household this article is designed to be of service in two ways. First, to direct the employment of certain measures towards the curing of the condition, and second, to warn the reader against the use of remedies which may be definitely harmful even though long custom has established a great vogue for them.

GETTING WELL

Rest— The First Essential

In the treatment of disease, a cardinal principle must be first realised. All that science and experience brings to the cure of certain conditions are merely auxiliaries to supplement Nature's efforts in quelling the ill-health. And the most important of Nature's weapons is *rest*. The highest form of this is undoubtedly peaceful sleep, when the energies of the body as a whole have ceased. During this period reparative changes are instituted, and a great reserve of energy is stored up. The cells of the body are refreshed and invigorated and are ready to continue battle with the invading disease. Medicine itself merely fortifies the body tissues against the onslaught. It is like an ammunition supply to an army, and can only be best employed if the soldiers

(the body cells) can handle the weapons (the medicines) successfully.

Local Rest

In lesser forms, local rest is employed —all with the same eventual purpose. A limb may be rested, a joint in the body may be fixed so that it is not used, a broken nervous system is sent on holiday so that the brain is not taxed, and so on.

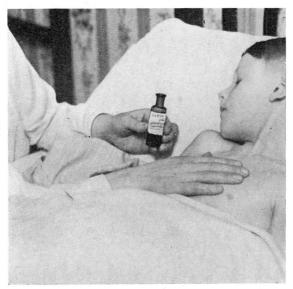

Fig. 1.—As a Remedy for Coughs, this is to be Condemned.

Rubbing the chest with camphorated oil is an old practice that is still common as a remedy for coughs and colds, especially for children. This article gives reasons why it is an unwise habit which should be discontinued.

A Suitable Environment for the Patient

The next principle to be grasped is that all the bodily functions are so attended to that they work at their best. For example, the stomach—there must be no over-eating, though, at the same time a sufficiency of nourishment must be provided. The skin must be kept clean and not over-covered, so that it may function at its highest efficiency. Plenty of fresh air should be provided, so that the body cells may be purified by contact with the pure oxygen it contains. Regular evacuations of the bowels should be effected so that no noxious residues are left behind to poison the patient.

Keep the Patient Cheerful

Finally, and not the least important, it is imperative to appreciate that the balance between life and death is frequently

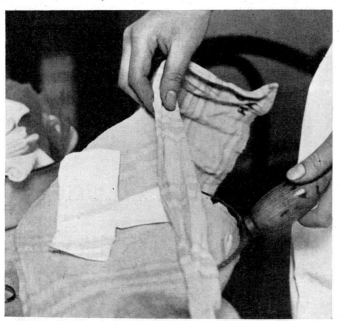

Fig. 2.—DEALING WITH CUTS THAT HAVE BECOME INFLAMED.
Shows the first stage in making a hot fomentation—rolling up a piece of lint that is to cover the inflamed part in a face towel.

Fig. 3.—TO MAKE A HOT FOMENTATION—SECOND STAGE.
Pour boiling water over the lint, which is rolled in the towel. The towel is then tightly wrung to squeeze out the water, leaving the lint as dry as possible.

dependent on the patient's will to come through. Everything should be done to encourage him. Though in the common disorders, such an issue is not likely to arise, yet even in an illness of minor gravity a cheerful outlook brings a quick convalescence.

DEALING WITH CUTS AND GRAZES

From the surgical aspect we have to deal with two groups of conditions :—

(*a*) Those due to injury, and

(*b*) Those the outcome of inflammation.

Don't Treat Cuts with Contempt.

Injuries to the skin are cuts or grazes. These are of such everyday occurrence that familiarity breeds a certain amount of contempt for the condition. Yet safety lies only in the direction of careful attention to the cleansing and purification of the affected parts.

Remove the Dirt

It is as well to remove all the superficial dirt and contamination present. If the injured part is dirtied the area *around* it should be carefully washed with soap and water. Should the cut extend deeply and should there be dirt at the edge of the wound, it would be better to get medical assistance to remove this rather than allow it to get into the depths by injudicious prodding. If there is bleeding, and this is superficial, it can be easily arrested by applying firmly a clean cloth to the surface of the wound. Should an antiseptic be at hand, such as iodine, it could be applied with advantage to the cut and the part covered over.

Stopping Bleeding

It sometimes happens that the bleeding may continue from a deep wound and the hæmorrhage may not be checked by these measures. In such cases, if the damaged part be a limb, a tightly-bound handkerchief or two above the cut will suffice to check it, especially if the limb is raised at the same time.

Cuts That Need Expert Attention

A cardinal point to bear in mind is that all penetrating wounds or wound infected with soil, garden manure, or street refuse, should receive expert attention from the hands of a doctor.

DEALING WITH INFLAMMATION

Next, let us consider inflammation. A cut may "fester," and the sore area will rapidly become red, hot and painful.

Should the Inflammation Keep Spreading

The ideal treatment for the condition is to *rest* the part. If it is the arm, put it into a sling ; if the leg, the patient is put to bed. But naturally such extreme measures will not often be needed.

Fomentations

The wounded area should be fomented, and if scabs tend to form these should be carefully removed after washing in hot water so that discharges do not collect underneath them. The fomentations should be used every four hours.

How to Prepare a Hot Fomentation

The best way to prepare the fomentation is to first take a piece of boracic lint of a size sufficient to cover the inflamed area with a margin to spare. Lay this piece of lint on to the edge of a face towel and roll up the two together, as shown.

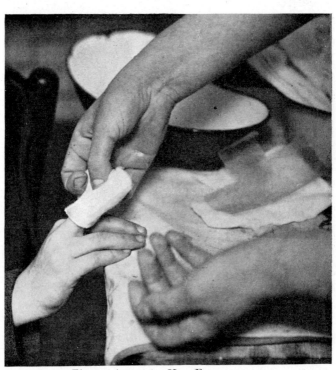

*Fig. 4.—*APPLYING HOT FOMENTATION.

After wringing out the water, as described in Fig. 3, the hot lint is then applied gently to the inflamed cut. Cover lint first with oil-silk, then a thick piece of cotton-wool, and bandage up.

Hold the two ends of the rolled-up towel and immerse the entire part where the lint lies into boiling water. Wring dry, then unroll the towel and gently apply the heated lint to the affected part. Take every care to see that the lint is practically dry or else any moisture left in it will tend to blister the part to which it is applied. Next cover the lint with a larger piece of green oil-silk, and over both apply a *thick* piece of cotton-wool to further retain the heat. Next bandage.

How to Remove Splinter under Finger Nail

The splinter under the nail is often encountered. If left there, very great inflammatory trouble can arise. Should medical help not be at hand a V-shaped sector of nail needs removing over the splinter, to permit of it being easily withdrawn by a pair of sharp-pointed

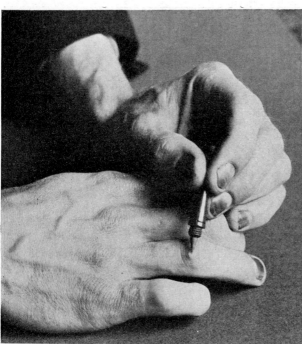

Fig. 5.—How to Get Rid of Warts.

Application of a silver nitrate stick on the wart every other day over a period of time will do what is needed. Moisten the wart before stroking it with the stick.

tweezers. Frequent fomentations should follow.

SKIN FORMATIONS

Eruptions in Children

The condition of impetigo in children yields to such treatment readily, especially if the scabs are removed by a saturated solution of soft soap in rectified spirit, and if afterwards the sores are treated with a 10 per cent. ichthyol ointment. Give the child a teaspoonful of

Parrish's food three times a day, in water before meals.

Treatment of Boils and Carbuncles

Boils and carbuncles are similarly treated. It should be remembered that the discharges must not be rubbed into or allowed to contaminate the adjoining areas, or else fresh trouble is sure to arise.

It should be recognised that occasionally sufferers from carbuncles may also be victims of diabetes, so that it is as well that such an associated condition should be excluded by necessary investigations.

Whitlows and Ingrowing Toenails

Infections about the fingers —popularly known as whitlows, and about the toes— ingrowing toenails, should always receive the very best medical attention, because they frequently become complicated by serious conditions leading to great disability and even to prolonged ill-health. They cannot be regarded as common disorders, and within the scope of this article.

Getting Rid of Warts

New formations, such as corns and warts, may be here considered. The latter yield to the application of the silver nitrate stick. This substance tends to burn surfaces it comes into contact with, so that three or four strokes with the stick on alternate days is all that is needful to cauterise the wart. At the same time care should be taken not to bring the substance into contact with clothing, which would otherwise be stained.

Cure of Corns

For the cure of corns, an ointment such as the following usually suffices :—
Acid salicylic, 1 dram.
Extract cannabis indica, 15 grains.
Flexible collodion to 1 ounce.

to three weeks to prevent flat foot following in the train of the injury.

MINOR AILMENTS

On the medical side there are numerous minor ailments that call for attention.

The Common Cold—Prevention with Vaccine Injection

The common cold is an everyday happening in the winter months in most households. Ideally, at the period of the greatest fitness of the individual— such as on the return from a holiday—an anticatarrh vaccine should be injected on two or three occasions as a prophylactic measure in preventing the onset of the attacks. Most doctors have advised this course with great benefit to chronic sufferers from this incapacitating condition.

Cure—With Ammoniated Tincture of Quinine

However, if the cold has occurred, the remedy most in vogue and one that is quite suitable is a teaspoonful dose of ammoniated tincture of quinine taken three times a day in water. Care should be observed in not persevering with this dosage should any giddiness or noises in the head occur. Combined with the quinine then taken, one drop of oil of cinnamon will also prove of great benefit if admixed.

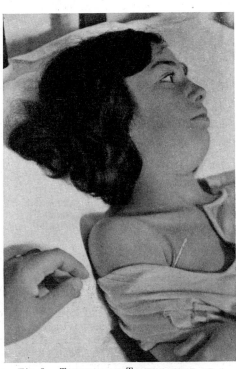

Fig. 8.—Taking the Temperature of a Patient.

Many persons, especially children, find it difficult to hold a clinical thermometer under the tongue, which is the usual way of taking the temperature of a patient. Another way is to place the bulb of the thermometer in the armpit. The elbows should be well pressed to the sides, so as to ensure good contact with the skin all round the mercury.

Other Aids to Cure

A hot drink before bedtime, a hot-water bottle, and a long night's rest are excellent aids. Generous dieting at such times considerably assists to overcome the infection, and great care should be taken to avoid exposure to the cold or wet before convalescence is completely established, as the susceptibility to pneumonia at this juncture is very great.

Coughing

It should be recognised that a cough frequently occurs at this stage. No medicine can be universally applicable for it, as it passes through various stages, needing the appropriate drugs at each stage to assist it. A doctor should therefore be consulted to advise what is most suitable.

An Old Remedy for Coughs—Not Recommended

There are a great many people, even to-day, who are addicted to the pernicious habit of rubbing the chest with camphorated oil, the purpose of which is to stimulate a patient to cough and also to provoke a secretion. This may be quite suitable in the very aged who have not the necessary vitality to cough sufficiently ; but it is unwise in the young to apply this stimulation, especially as it is frequently employed at a stage of the trouble when the cough is very dry and coughing only tends to make the chest more sore and aggravate the condition.

Paving the Way for Consumption

Further, it is believed that a chest which is full of secretion is an excellent nest for the germs of tuberculosis or consumption.

HEADACHES

Headaches are another common ailment which cause quite an amount of unnecessary distress. The causes are numerous, but an indication of these might prove invaluable in elucidating the origin of the trouble.

Caused by Defective Eyesight

First in the list must be placed defective eyesight. Advice in all cases of persistent headaches should be therefore sought from the hands of the most competent ophthalmic surgeon available, because frequently the defect in vision may be a very slight one indeed, yet the results may be most distressing.

Due to Bilious Attack

Secondly, especially in children, where it is accompanied with vomiting, there is the so-called bilious attack. The patient should be made to consume larger quantities of sugar than in the past. Glucose, especially in the form of barley sugar sticks, answers admirably, and a quarter of an ounce of this foodstuff should be included in the daily dietary.

Deranged Digestion a Cause

Thirdly, the digestive tract may be responsible. Great care of the bowels and the avoidance of indigestion should be the aims.

Headaches due to Nervous Complaints

In the fourth group are people who suffer from nervous headaches, and also those whose headaches are reflexes from an infected area about the head. These latter should consult their doctors, so that a thorough investigation will lead to the cause and the appropriate treatment.

CONSTIPATION

Constipation is another defect of everyday life which brings a great deal of ill-health in its train.

The Easiest Remedy

The easiest remedy, but one which is so often received contemptuously, is the regular drinking of at least one and a half pints of water daily. If expense is not a consideration, certain mineral spring waters are potent remedies for the evil, and should be employed.

What to Attend to

The cultivation of a regular habit of evacuation, and the avoidance of neglecting the desire, no matter how feeble, are next in importance.

And What to Avoid

Purgatives should be avoided. Aloes especially, as it has a predilection in causing piles. Exercises, for preference of the vigorous kind, and abdominal massage, all have their uses.

Another Simple Remedy

A simple remedy, and one which is not habit-forming, is the taking of a tablespoonful of liquid paraffin mixed in a tumbler of water, *with* the principal meal of the day. Should this amount be insufficient it needs augmenting till such a quantity is taken to ensure regularity. If a leakage of the oil occurs it is essential to *cut down* the regular dosage to the necessary limits to obviate this and to persist with the lesser dose.

Treatment of Piles

Whilst dealing with this question, a few words of advice on the treatment of piles would not be out of place. The best means of dealing with this evil is to create a soft and smooth motion such as that brought about by the use of liquid paraffin. After the motion has been voided care should be directed so as to avoid injury to the local area by the misuse of cleansing agents. Soap and water and cotton-wool, together with effective drying, meet the requirements ideally. If the piles are protruded they should be smeared with vaseline and pushed inside again. Each night a suppository, such as the following, should be inserted into the bowel, as far in as comfort permits, and allowed to dissolve in this site.

Bismuth subgallate grains, ten in a sufficiency of cocoa-butter to form a suppository.

Resinol ointment is one that would answer, frequently applied.

MAKING A RUSH-TOP STOOL

USEFUL and picturesque in appearance, the rush-top stool, shown in Fig. 1, can be made at home by anyone, and without tools of any kind.

The stool frame is obtainable assembled ready for staining and seating; the seagrass or rush is supplied in hanks ready for use. Two colours are preferable; about $\frac{1}{2}$lb. of brown and $\frac{1}{4}$ lb. of orange will suffice for a stool (as shown in Fig. 2), measuring 12 inches wide, 14 inches long, and 11$\frac{1}{2}$ inches high. The only other materials required are a small quantity of wood filler paste, or a small knob of whiting; a small quantity of dark-oak water stain, and a gill of french polish.

Preparing the Seat Frame

Commence the work by sandpapering the whole of the seat frame until it is perfectly smooth, then dissolve the wood filler,

Fig. 1.—Rush-Top Stool.
This handy article can be made by anyone who follows the clear instructions in the text.

or the knob of whiting, in water to form a creamy paste, and rub this while wet into the grain of the wood; allow it to dry, rub it down with sandpaper, remove all dust, then brush it all over with dark-oak wood stain; allow it to dry, rub down very lightly with sandpaper, then brush it over with the french polish. Again leave it to dry, then very lightly remove any roughness with sandpaper.

In the photographs the four sides of the frame have been left bright and lettered A, B, C, D for the purposes of reference and identification.

Commencing the Seating

The rush pattern is worked in the following manner: Lay the brown seagrass alongside the inside edge of the frame at A, then bring the seagrass over the side B, under it and up and over side A, thus binding

Fig. 2.—Parts for the Stool.
Necessary materials are the stool frame and three-quarters of a pound of seagrass, seen in this illustration.

Fig. 3.—COMMENCING THE SEATING.
This photographic diagram shows the manner in which the seagrass is
worked on the frame.

the starting end to the frame.

Then take the seagrass under the side A, over side C, then down under it, up and over side B, down and under it, then over side D, down and under it, up over and under C, and then over A, down and under it, up and over side D, down and under it, then come up and over the side B next to the first strand. The positions of the seagrass at this stage are shown in Fig. 3, and exactly the same proceeding is continued until twelve

Fig. 4.—CLOSE-UP DETAIL OF RUSH PATTERN.
The manner in which the strands interlace and
form a mitre at the corners is clearly shown.

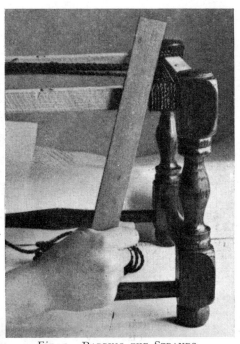

Fig. 5.—RAPPING THE STRANDS.
The strands are pressed closely together with
a rapping iron or with a flat boxwood ruler used in
the manner of a hammer, as here shown.

complete strands have been worked.

Take care to form the corner mitre, seen in Fig. 4, as neatly as possible, also press the strands closely together by knocking them with a rapping iron, or with a boxwood ruler (as shown in Fig. 5), using it in the manner of a hammer.

Forming the Pattern

Variety is given to the seat by working the next twelve strands with the orange seagrass, which forms an L-shape near each corner, then continue until finished with the brown seagrass.

It is most convenient to use the seagrass in lengths of about 8 yards, rolled up into a ball, and to join the ends, where necessary, with a reef knot, bringing it on the underside of the

Fig. 6.—KNOTTING THE SEAGRASS.

The ends of the seagrass are fastened together with a reef knot, tied so that it comes on the underside of the seat. The knot is here shown with a piece of card behind it to reveal the details.

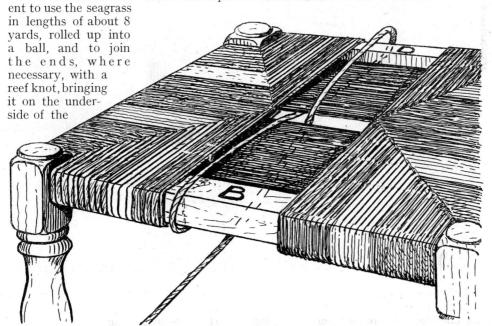

Fig. 7.—FINISHING THE SEATING.

When the shorter sides of the stool have been filled, the space on the longer sides is completed by working the seagrass in a figure-of-eight manner.

Fig. 8.—STAGES IN TYING THE REEF KNOT.
Three stages in tying the reef knot, showing the proper way of ensuring
a good joint.

the diagram Fig. 7), commencing from the top of side B, then down through the centre under the seat, up and over side D, then down through the centre, under the seat, up and over side B, and so on. Press the seagrass very closely together in

seat (as seen in Fig. 6), and tying the knot as shown in the diagram Fig. 8, where it will be seen that, when completed, the knot is virtually a pair of interlaced loops and can never slip.

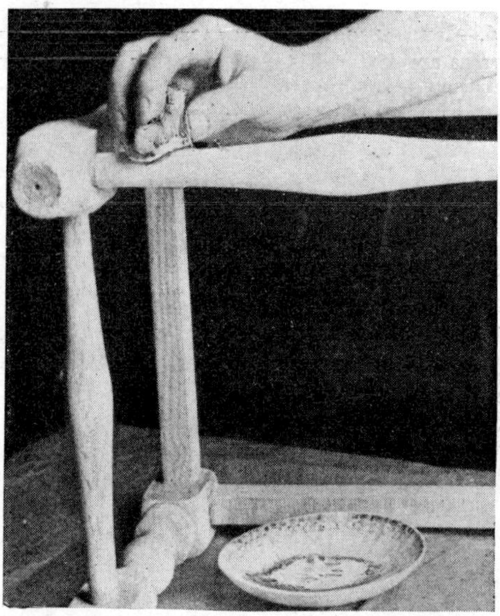

the centre, keep all strands tight and uniformly spaced, then finish off by knotting the end two or three times to strands on the opposite side of and underneath the seat.

Fig. 9.—FILLING THE GRAIN.
After sandpapering the wood to make it smooth, the pores of the grain are closed with a paste filler rubbed in with a pad of rag.

Fig. 10.—BRUSHING ON THE STAIN.
A pleasing colour is imparted by brushing the wood with a dark-brown water stain. The wood can then be polished as described in the text.

Completing the Stool

As the frame is not equal-sided, the shorter ends are filled in before the longer sides, and from that stage the seating is completed by threading the seagrass in a figure-of-eight manner (as shown in

Complete the stool by pressing any overriding strands into their places, and impart a pleasing gloss to the frame by brushing it with french polish and finishing off with a rubber dipped in the polish and worked lightly but briskly over the surfaces.